The Lion of Judah

Other Ariel Biographies

The Lion of Judah

A life of
Haile Selassie I
Emperor of Ethiopia
·
Charles Gorham

Ariel Books

FARRAR, STRAUS
& GIROUX

Copyright © 1966 by Charles Gorham
Library of Congress catalog card number 66–11707
All rights reserved
First printing, 1966
Ariel Books, a division of Farrar, Straus and Giroux
Published simultaneously in Canada by
Ambassador Books, Ltd., Toronto
Printed in the United States of America by H. Wolff, New York

Contents

The Lion of Judah

1

Geneva, 1936

On the last day of June, 1936, in the pretty Swiss city
of Geneva, cooled by the breezes of the lovely lake,
the delegates of fifty-two countries seated themselves
uneasily in the vast assembly hall of the League of
Nations, unsuccessful ancestor of our United Nations. With the exception of the United States, which
was not a member, almost every civilized country in
the world was represented. The press galleries were
filled with reporters. The League of Nations, founded

after World War I, was being put to the test by a small and half-forgotten country whose very existence had been snuffed out by the guns and the bombs of Italian Fascist troopers. The honor of the civilized world was at stake.

There was a silence in the great hall, broken only by an awkward cough and the occasional shuffling of feet. A slim, bearded, dark-faced figure was escorted to the speaker's platform. He was dressed in white, a black cape over his shoulders. The face was calm, the hands slim and poetic. There was about him a sense of majesty upon which many had remarked. He was a king and he looked like a king. His bearing was regal, almost austere, and his dignity brought total silence to the great chamber. The delegates rose as a mark of respect. Haile Selassie I, Emperor of Ethiopia, King of Kings, Conquering Lion of the Tribe of Judah, had come to the court of international justice to plead for the very life of his country.

From the press gallery, Italian journalists shouted insults and obscenities at the tragic and lonely figure on the rostrum. They were removed by the guards and order was restored. In a low voice, using his native Amharic, the Emperor spoke:

"I, Haile Selassie I, Emperor of Ethiopia, am here today to claim that justice is due to my people . . ."

He told the delegates how the Italian armies had invaded his country, in violation of all international

treaties. He told of the terror that had rained from
the skies, for the Fascist airmen (one of them the son
of Mussolini himself) had used poison gas as well as
bombs.

"Men and animals succumbed. The deadly rain
that fell from the aircraft made all those whom it
touched fly, shrieking with pain. All who drank the
poisoned water or ate the infected food succumbed
too, in dreadful suffering. In tens of thousands, the
victims of the Italian mustard gas died. It was to denounce to the civilized world the tortures inflicted
upon the Ethiopian people that I resolved to come
to Geneva . . ."

Today the world is hardened to the idea of bombardment from the air. We live in the presence of
rockets ready to bear atomic death to the far cities
of the earth. When the Emperor spoke at Geneva
more than a generation ago, only his country had
suffered the full force of terror from the skies. What
had happened in Ethiopia was a rehearsal for things
to come. In his quiet voice, speaking almost without
passion, the dark-faced monarch was giving the delegates at Geneva a forecast of what would happen if
the world now chose to ignore the brutal invasion of
his country.

"Apart from the Kingdom of God," he said, "no
nation on this earth is higher than any other. If a
strong government can destroy a weak people, then
the hour has struck for all weak peoples. I appeal to

the League of Nations to give its judgment in all freedom. God and history will remember your judgment . . ."

When the Emperor finished, there were tears in the eyes of some of the delegates. Representatives of small nations shuddered with fear for their own future. But the great free nations of the world were afraid. They thought they could buy peace from Mussolini if only they permitted him to take Ethiopia. And they were afraid of Adolf Hitler, whose ruthless armies were already forming, whose Luftwaffe was soon to be tested in the sky over the placid Spanish town of Guernica.

The great governments mumbled regrets.

Haile Selassie left Geneva, going to England, to the city of Bath, to begin a long and bitter exile. Many years were to pass and all the world was to be scorched by war before the solemn and sturdy Emperor was again to set foot in his own country, which had been the last free nation in all of Africa, except for tiny Liberia.

In exile, Haile Selassie suffered insult and disappointment. He lost his power and the right to rule his country and much of the prestige he had enjoyed. But three things he never lost. These were his pride, his courage, and his faith. For he was a Christian king, of the ancient line of Solomon, and a sense of destiny burned within him. He was content to wait on the judgment of God. He drew strength from the ancient line of kings who had for so many centuries—for two thousand years and more—maintained the independence of their strange and mysterious mountain nation.

He was patient and he trusted God, but as he left the hall at Geneva, he could not resist murmuring to those who had turned their backs on his country: "It is us today; it will be you tomorrow."

And to many people, looking back today, it was the invasion of Ethiopia that truly began the long, dark years of war that made the world a place of terror and brought death to so many millions. For proud France in the end was to watch with tears an invading army marching through the sweet streets of Paris, and proud Great Britain was to be shaken by months of savage bombardment.

If the great powers had responded to Haile Selassie's appeal for help, would the war have been avoided? We do not know. But we do know that in the end his warning proved to be correct. *"It is us today; it will be you tomorrow."* How many men who sat in Geneva and heard the Emperor's warning must remember his words today?

But in those days, in their minds, he was another African king, a black man from a black man's country, not worth defending, even with words.

2

The seed of King Solomon

In the streets of Addis Ababa, the mountain capital of Ethiopia, the traveler will be offered scenes painted on canvas depicting important events from the Ethiopian epic, the *Kebra Negast*—"The Glory of Kings."

The *Kebra Negast* is old and the story it tells is older. In Ethiopia it is of great political importance. Upon the legend of the *Kebra Negast* is based the right of the Kings of Ethiopia to rule their dark-skinned subjects, who have been independent since the days of the Old Testament, cut off from the rest of Africa, as Tibet has been cut off from the world, by the towering, magnificent, and frightening mountains that make up a good share of the country.

Here is the story which is told in the *Kebra Negast* and which school boys in Ethiopia learn along with the ABC's of the strange Amharic alphabet:

The Queen of Sheba—the Queen of the South—ruled a country on the Red Sea in part of what is now Arabia. She had heard of the wisdom and splendor of Solomon, the mighty ruler of the Land of the Jews. She was determined to see for herself the magnificence of Solomon's kingdom, and she journeyed from her own country to his royal court, bearing gifts and armed by her own famous beauty, for she was then considered one of the most beautiful women in the world.

She was not disappointed. All that she had heard of the glory of Solomon's court was true. He was indeed the greatest of all the kings in the world and the Queen of Sheba remained at his side, asking for his advice so that she could return to her own country and govern with equal wisdom and splendor.

Solomon would gladly have made her his queen, for he was delighted by her beauty and grace, but she felt that her duty demanded that she remain with her own people. However, for a time she did become the companion of great King Solomon and she bore him a son. According to the *Kebra Negast,* this was Solomon's first-born son. He was named Ibn Hakim and his father gave him a jeweled ring, by means of which he could prove to the world his descent from the ruler of the Land of the Jews. According to the *Kebra Negast,* "his whole body and its members and the bearing of his shoulders resembled those of King Solomon his father."

And so was established the line of kings who rule Ethiopia today, for the people of the Queen of Sheba crossed the Red Sea from Arabia and established themselves in the high mountains beyond the plain on the western coast. And so it is from Solomon, King of the Jews, that His Imperial Majesty, Haile Selassie I, King of the Kings of Ethiopia, Conquering Lion of Judah, is supposed to have been descended. Between Solomon and Haile Selassie stands a line of 323 kings, giving the Ethiopians some claim to possessing the oldest monarchy in the world.

It is a strange story, romantically clouded by the mists of time. According to students of ancient history, it may not be altogether true in the strictest literal sense. But it is symbolically true, and probably there is real truth in it, for there must have been some sort of conquest in ancient times to account for the Semitic character of the leading race of Ethiopia and the Semitic form of the official language, Amharic, the characters of which resemble the Hebrew.

The land that is ruled by Haile Selassie might well have attracted people who lived in the lowland countries along the shores of the Red Sea, where the land is apt to be mostly desert and the heat as bad as that of the Arizona desert in midsummer. On the high plateau of Ethiopia, heart of the country, the mountains rise majestically and the days are pleasantly warm, despite the fact that the Equator is near. The nights are cool and sometimes cold. Addis Ababa, the modern capital, now sparkling with neon lights, is high in the mountains, at 8,000 feet, and strangers find that the altitude makes their hearts beat faster and sometimes at first they gasp for breath.

Even today, most of the country is rich mountain jungle. There are giant podocarpus trees, with trunks seven feet in diameter. There are mimosa and the fragrant pencil cedar and, in modern times, the fragrant eucalyptus. There is wild game of all kinds: lions, leopards, cheetahs, lynx, and everywhere the savage hyena, with jaws so powerful they can crush the leg of an elephant. There are baboons and, in the trees, a pretty black and white monkey. There are gazelles and even giraffes.

The country of Haile Selassie, which today includes the former Italian coastal colony of Eritrea, dominates the so-called Horn of Africa, the land mass that juts out into the Red Sea. In area it is larger than France and Germany taken together, but the population (there has never been a census) is probably not more than 20 million.

Ethiopia has never been a nation in the sense that England and France are nations. Within Haile Selassie's borders, more than seventy languages are spoken. There are four great racial groups and many sub-tribes. The dominant race are the Amharas, who live in the northern part of the Empire. By government command their language, Amharic, is rapidly being made universal. It is the language of the court and of the Emperor himself, though of course he is also at ease in French and English.

To the south of the powerful Amhara group live the Galla warriors, whose girls are among the most beautiful in the world. To the southeast and in the desert regions live the fierce Danakils and many tribesmen from Somaliland. The fourth large group are the Shankalla, who are Negroid in appearance, and resemble the Negroes to be seen in Europe and the United States.

There remain the Falasha, or Ethiopian Jews. The name Falasha means exile, and these people, who live to the north of the great Lake Tsana, believe themselves destined to return to the Promised Land of the Bible. Though they practice the Jewish religion, their scriptures are not in Hebrew but in the ancient Geez language that is used by the Coptic Church of Ethiopia. Each Jewish community has its Megid, or synagogue, and its Kahan, or rabbi.

Such then are the Ethiopians, the "mingling of the races," that is mentioned in the Bible. Until modern times the country was feudal, ruled by all-powerful local chiefs and war lords, who to this day bear the name Ras, a title roughly equivalent to Prince or Duke. Haile Selassie, as we shall see, was Ras Tafari before he ascended the Imperial throne.

Who could rule this assortment of people, many of them almost savage, hating the stranger and detesting all authority? Only a great man, to be sure, and during the last century Ethiopia's first great modern ruler appeared. He was called Menelik, a fearless warrior and a wise leader. With his comrade-in-arms, Ras Makonnen, Menelik defeated the Italian armies at Adowa in 1896, a defeat the Italians never forgot and were later to avenge against Haile Selassie. When the Italian army invaded his country, Menelik buckled on his sword. "Let him that is strong follow me; and let him who is weak pray for us and for success to our arms." With these words he took to the field. Ninety thousand Ethiopian warriors followed him, to meet the army of Italy. When the battle was over, 12,000 Italians had been killed and 4,000 taken prisoner. Ethiopia was saved from invasion.

On the battlefield at Adowa, Menelik threw his arms around Ras Makonnen, who had been the bravest of all his comrades.

"We have fought together like father and son," he said to Ras Makonnen. "Like father and son we shall be from this day forth."

Ras Makonnen said nothing, but he understood what King Menelik meant. Menelik had no sons. He intended to reward Ras Makonnen with the throne, when the time came for him to die, for they were related, and Ras Makonnen too was of the Seed of Solomon.

Ras Makonnen was soon to become the father of Haile Selassie I, but for the son of Ras Makonnen the road to the throne in Addis Ababa was to be long, hard, and dangerous.

But triumphant.

3

The birth of Haile Selassie

Impatiently, Ras Makonnen waited for the news, striding nervously back and forth, his broad warrior's shoulders swaying as he walked, his long, jeweled cape flowing behind him.

"It must be a boy!" his mind told him, as his great fist struck his palm. "It must be a son!"

For Ras Makonnen had no son, and if he was to inherit the throne of Menelik, which he had won on the field of battle, he wanted an heir to stand behind him, a boy he could raise to rule the country and bring the nation forward into the modern world, to complete the work that Menelik had so ably started.

Ras Makonnen's wife, Lady Yeshimabeit, was not in the city of Harar, capital of the province ruled by Ras Makonnen, for the warm weather had set in and the family had been moved to Ejarsa Gorsa, high on a green hillside that overlooked the rich and fertile valleys of Makonnen's domain, the land given to him to rule as a reward for his bravery against the Italians at Adowa.

So it was at Ejarsa Gorsa, in Ras Makonnen's summer house, built of mud and wattle, with a broad, cool verandah, that Haile Selassie was born. While his mother waited, outside the big house the village women prayed and loo-looed in their curious manner, a soft, humming, musical sound. Almost at the instant of the boy's birth, the hillsides shuddered under heavy thunder. The sound rolled away like artillery in the distance and then the dark skies burst and the rain came down in torrents. In a country where rain is always needed, the storm was taken as a sign that the newborn infant was especially blessed. The women loo-looed and offered thanks to God. The baby's lips were moistened with ritual butter. In the little village of Ejarsa Gorsa, hill tribesmen fired their rifles in celebration. The Coptic priests offered prayers. For two nights there was a feast at Ras Makonnen's expense, the villagers devouring the strips of raw meat that they loved, cutting toward themselves with sharp knives. They drank their fill of *tej* and *talla*, the national drinks of Ethiopia.

"Ras Makonnen has a son!" the villagers chanted at the feast of celebration. "Praise be to God!"

For Ras Makonnen was a good ruler and well-loved in the Province of Harar, respected for his bravery as a soldier as well as for his fairness as a governor. He had brought peace to the Province of Harar and some prosperity to the people, as well as justice to the provincial courts, and these were things that most Ethiopian Rases in those days did not trouble to think about.

A month after Haile Selassie was born, he and his mother were carried to the walled city of Harar, where Ras Makonnen waited at the city gate. They were borne on richly ornamented litters, protected from the sun by brightly colored ceremonial umbrellas. Outriders in brilliant costumes, leopard and lion skins on their shoulders, led the way and brought up the rear. Men shouted and fired their rifles into the air. The women chanted softly. At every hamlet along the way, chiefs brought out refreshment, while humble people came out of their tukuls, or mud huts, to bow their heads in respect. If none of them suspected that the babe being carried toward Harar was one day to be their Emperor, at least they knew that he was a prince and the son of the man who, next to King Menelik himself, was the most important and powerful chief in all of Ethiopia.

Outside the walls of the fortified city, Ras Makonnen waited for the procession to arrive. He took his son in his arms and carried him on horseback through the main gate of the ancient city. He raised his eyes to Almighty God and offered a little prayer of thanks. Then, with the boy on the pommel of his richly ornamented saddle, he galloped toward the Governor's Palace, through narrow, medieval streets that were lined with his cheering subjects.

"Tafari, my son," he murmured to the child. "One day you will be king, and King of Kings."

For though his baptismal name was Haile Selassie, in accordance with Ethiopian custom, the future Emperor was called by another name, and during the early years of his life he was to be known as Lij Tafari, or Tafari Makonnen, the title Lij meaning, more or less, prince or person of royal blood. A more suitable name than Tafari could hardly have been found for him, for in Amharic the word means "Without Fear" and in years to come, Lij Tafari was many times to prove his right to bear the name.

Ras Makonnen had good reason to thank God for the birth of his son. Two years later, his wife was again with child and this time she died. The rearing of little Lij Tafari was left entirely to his father. His early education and religious instruction were in the hands of the family confessor, Aba Walda Kidan. It was this priest who taught the boy his catechism and taught him too the Amharic alphabet, odd letters related to those of old-style Hebrew.

In those days there were no schools, even for the sons of the rich and well-born. Education did not go very far. Most of the Rases scorned learning. Somehow, in their minds, reading and writing were tied up with the *ferengi,* the foreigners, who were feared and hated. Haile Selassie's education normally would have stopped with a smattering of Amharic and a slight knowledge of the Coptic religion.

But in 1902, when Lij Tafari was ten, Ras Makonnen was sent to London to represent Ethiopia at the Coronation of King Edward VII, son of Queen Victoria. He was impressed by what he saw in the glittering capital of Great Britain and he was shrewd enough to understand that education was the key to the future, if Ethiopia was to come out of the Middle Ages and enter the modern world. When he returned to Harar in September of 1902, he sought out Doctor Vitalien, who had been brought from the French island of Guadeloupe to open a hospital in Harar.

"I want my son to learn French," Ras Makonnen told the good doctor. "I know that you are busy at the hospital, but try to spare him an hour a day."

What Doctor Vitalien could not do was done by a tutor provided by Monsignor Jarosseau of the French Catholic Mission at Harar, a certain Aba Samuel. And so the first foreign language studied by Lij Tafari, future king, was the supple, logical, and beautiful language of France. If it is true that in a sense language helps to form character, perhaps some of the clarity and precision later to be shown by Haile Selassie came from the fact that when he was small he mastered his honest French verbs and drank in the logic of the French language.

He learned other things too.

He learned that his country was backward, without roads or schools or railways or proper hospitals. Each year, hundreds of thousands of his countrymen were bought and sold as slaves. The Rases and priests who controlled the country were ignorant and often proud to be ignorant. In the misery that he saw around him, young Lij Tafari saw his life work. From the time he was very young, perhaps even as early as when he was seven, he seems somehow to have known in his heart that he would one day be ruler of his native land. He had that awareness of destiny that so often seems given at birth to those whose fate it is to be powerful and great. Napoleon had it. So had Alexander the Great. So did Hitler and Mussolini. Used for good, this conviction of a destiny to rule can offer much to the world. Used for evil, it can bring the world to ruin. Lij Tafari, Haile Selassie, from the beginning seems to have been determined to bring progress to his country and to help to bring peace to the world.

When Lij Tafari was eleven, the Emperor Menelik sent for him. He wanted to see the son of the friend he intended to make his successor. Ras Makonnen took the boy to the capital at Addis Ababa and Lij Tafari stood in the splendor of the great court, in the center of the Imperial Palace. Royal lions, symbol of the Imperial power, paced on silent feet in the open yard of the palace. Menelik sat on a high throne, a sober, brooding figure, his face adorned with a short beard. Around him were soldiers of the Imperial Guard, lion skins on their shoulders, headdresses made of lions' manes.

Lij Tafari wore a velvet hat, white knee breeches, a cloak of black silk embroidered with gold. He was small for his age, and delicate, but already there was an expression of strength in his eyes and his face showed keen intelligence.

"So you can speak French and read it too," the Emperor Menelik said to Tafari. "Let us hear you perform, my boy."

Lij Tafari bowed to his sovereign and recited a fable of La Fontaine. Menelik was a great man, but he did not know a word of French. When Tafari had finished, Menelik roared with laughter.

"He has learned it by heart," he protested to Ras

Makonnen. "He doesn't really know what the words mean."

Makonnen smiled; he had his reports from Doctor Vitalien and the Aba Samuel.

"Speak to Monsieur Ilg, my son," he said quietly to Tafari.

Tafari turned to the Swiss engineer who was attached as adviser to Menelik's court. The man and the boy conversed in French while Menelik and his court looked on and listened. After a little, Ilg nodded. The great Menelik was satisfied. The son of his friend and comrade-in-arms actually could speak French. He and his court burst into applause.

"You have done well, my boy," Menelik said to Tafari. "You will have much to give our country."

Menelik and his courtiers were impressed, but there were two people in the great throne room who looked at young Lij Tafari with hatred and suspicion. One was Menelik's Queen, Taitu, who hated Ras Makonnen and who wanted herself to replace Menelik, to become the first reigning Empress since the Queen of Sheba. The other was a tough old war lord, Ras Mikael. He was married to one of Menelik's daughters and he too had a son, Lij Yasu. At that moment, Tafari and Yasu had never met, but already they were bitter rivals, each in his own way a candidate for the throne. They were as different from one another as two boys can be. Tafari was serious, given to thought, deeply religious, and patriotic. Lij Yasu was insolent, cruel, and reckless. If Tafari belonged to the future, Lij Yasu belonged to the past, and in Ethiopia the past had often been dark and cruel for the people. The fate of Ethiopia in a sense depended on the outcome of the struggle between these two boys.

A few months after he returned to Harar, Lij Tafari learned that the Emperor Menelik had awarded him the title of Dejazmach—"Keeper of the Door."

It was a great honor for one so young.

Ras Makonnen took Tafari aside and said to him, "I have made you my heir."

In Ethiopia, sons do not automatically succeed to the lands, titles, and riches of their fathers. The father must select his heir, and sometimes he does not select his son. There is no doubt that Ras Makonnen made Tafari his heir because he knew that soon Menelik would announce that he, Makonnen, was to be the heir of the Emperor Menelik himself, and that when the Emperor Menelik died, Ras Makonnen would enter Addis Ababa to become the next King of Kings.

Certainly this was what Menelik wanted. There was no man in all of Ethiopia so loved and trusted by Menelik as his old war comrade, Ras Makonnen. "As father and son we have fought," he had said, on the field at Adowa. "As father and son we shall live."

For Makonnen and Lij Tafari, the road to the crown seemed safe and sure, but in April of 1906, when Lij Tafari was fourteen, Ras Makonnen was taken ill and died. A certain mystery surrounds his death. In those days, Ethiopian Rases usually died in battle, or from luxurious living, or from the rigors of the constant religious fasting demanded by the Coptic Church. Ras Makonnen was a strong soldier and correct in his personal habits. He did not indulge in the excesses of drink and debauchery that carried off many of his fellow princes.

Could he have been poisoned by agents of his enemies, Queen Taitu or Ras Mikael?

No one knows.

But when Ras Makonnen died, two candidates for the Imperial throne were removed from the contest, Makonnen himself and his son Tafari. Certainly Queen Taitu and Ras Mikael must have been happy to learn of Ras Makonnen's death.

So was Lij Yasu. Already, though only a boy, he was beginning to show signs of the ruthless ambition and cruelty that were to appear later in their full horror. As a young man, Lij Yasu was to come near to ruining his country.

Menelik remained loyal to Tafari, son of his old friend, but he too was ill and subject to pressure from his Queen. A half-brother, Yilma, was appointed Governor of Harar instead of Tafari.

"Tafari is too young," the Queen insisted, and Menelik gave in.

Tafari was brought to Addis Ababa to remain for a time at Menelik's side. He was appointed governor of the tiny province of Solali, but it was an honorary post and a deputy actually governed the province while Tafari remained at Menelik's court. There, in the midst of medieval intrigue, where dark plots and even murder were the order of the day, the future Emperor Haile Selassie was to attend a hard school and one in which he learned how to survive in the political life of the jungle that was to come to Ethiopia when Menelik died.

"I have founded a school, so that our young men may be trained to deal with the rest of the world," the Emperor Menelik told Tafari, soon after the boy arrived in Addis Ababa. "You must become one of the first pupils. Work, learn, study. The country needs you."

Lij Tafari did not need to be urged to continue his education. He was thirsty for knowledge, hungry for books. He studied languages, history, religion, even economics. At Menelik's court he studied the hearts and the minds of men. And women. For in the background there was always his enemy, Queen Taitu, and she became more and more powerful as Menelik's health continued to fail.

The Imperial court was grand. There were silks

and satins in the rich hall. There were china plates from Sèvres in France, embossed with the emblem of the Lion of Judah. The courtiers dressed in rich clothing. For foreign guests there were wines of the finest vintages, brought from Europe. Outside the walls of the palace, things were different. The capital city itself was not much more than a mud village. Addis Ababa (in Amharic the words mean "New Flower") had been founded less than a generation before Tafari became a member of Menelik's court. The city was a disorganized collection of mud huts, or tukuls, with the Imperial buildings at the center. There were no roads leading into the town, only rough mule tracks. There were almost no streets, simply footpaths leading from one tiny circular house to another. The city stands at an altitude of 8,000 feet (nearly three thousand feet higher than Denver), and the air is bracing. In dry weather, in spite of its raw newness and the desperate poverty in its back alleys, Addis Ababa was not unpleasant, for there was the beauty of the blue Entoto Mountains, which fell away in the distance, and the majesty of the eucalyptus forests, great trees imported by Menelik from Australia and planted on the hillsides near the capital so that the city should not run short of firewood. The mountain air was fragrant, as it is today, with the scent of eucalyptus and spices —frankincense and myrrh, the smells of the Old Testament.

When the rainy season started, however, the city became a great mud flat, cold and miserable, the rutted streets impassable. During the day, garbage was piled up in the streets. At night the gates of the city were opened to hyenas, who devoured the heaps of refuse. These dangerous, spotted beasts were the city's only sanitation system.

Menelik had made an effort to abolish slavery and slave auctions were against the law, but there were slaves in every rich household and outside the city there were secret places where, for a few Maria Theresa talers, one could buy a pretty Galla girl or a sturdy Danakil laborer. Even a prosperous small farmer often owned a slave or two, and the system went on, unchecked, as it had since the days before the Birth of Christ.

When he was a boy of fifteen and sixteen, attending the Menelik School in Addis, Lij Tafari saw these things. In his mind and heart great plans were growing. He looked at the mud huts and the slave markets, at the primitive mule tracks that led into the capital, at his countrymen living in poverty, and he went into the great church to pray. To pray and to promise to God that he, Tafari, Haile Selassie, would one day change all this. He would build a modern city, with paved streets, electric lights, schools, even a university. He would free the slaves and see to it that they had the chance really to become free men. He would do away with the ancient biblical system of justice—an eye for an eye, a tooth for a tooth—in which a thief's hand was cut off at the wrist in the public square, and replace this system with modern courts of justice.

Tafari was the most brilliant student at the Menelik School. Also, though slight of build, with the face of a poet, he was fearless and able to conceal pain, always a virtue in Ethiopia. One day, he and Menelik, with others of the Imperial court, were riding on the plain outside Addis Ababa. Tafari's horse stepped into a pothole, stumbled, and Tafari was thrown from the saddle. Behind him his rival, Lij Yasu, burst into contemptuous laughter. The rest of the royal party giggled. Tafari remounted and Lij Yasu trotted up beside him.

"Come, cousin, let us race," he said arrogantly.

Tafari spurred his horse and shot away like a bullet. In front of the Emperor and the royal entourage, he gave an exhibition of horsemanship that made everyone gasp. Even Lij Yasu for once was silent and bit his lip in anger, reining in his own horse. He could not compete with Tafari.

When the party returned to the palace, it was discovered that when he was thrown, Tafari had broken his wrist. Yet during his exhibition of riding he had not shown a sign of pain. His face had remained calm and serene. Menelik stood by while the broken bone was set. He patted Tafari's shoulder.

"They call you 'The Shy One,' " the Emperor said. "But you have the spirit of an eagle, the courage of a lion."

Menelik had a problem. He wanted to name Tafari his heir, but he knew that to do this would place Tafari's life in danger. Both the Queen and Ras Mikael would stop at nothing to prevent Tafari from becoming King. It was best to wait, Menelik decided. To wait until his own death was closer.

Still, the boy must not be wasted. He was seventeen. It was time for him to take his place somewhere in the government of the Empire.

"You shall be Governor of Sidamo," Menelik said. "It will be your real school, now that the classrooms are behind you."

In those days it was unheard of for an Ethiopian to go abroad to study at a foreign university. When he had finished at the Menelik School, Tafari's education came to an end. He bowed his head in thanks.

"After Sidamo, who knows?" Menelik asked softly. "You are young but you will govern well, as your father governed before you."

And so, traveling with a mule train, flanked by horsemen armed with rifles, Tafari left Addis Ababa and rode through the dizzying mountain passes to the province that had been placed under his command. He entered manhood at seventeen, with all the power of a feudal lord, with the power of life and death over the men and women in his new domain. Also, and he knew it, he had the power to change their lives for the better, to make of Sidamo a model province, to go even further than his father had gone, when Ras Makonnen had been Governor of Harar. He had never been a boaster like Lij Yasu, but there was no false modesty in him either. He felt his own strength and he trusted his own power.

4

The young ruler

Sidamo is a rich and fertile southern province. It
touches the borders of Kenya, now a great African
republic, at that time part of the British Empire.
Sidamo is situated on a high plateau, most of the
land being at an altitude of 6,000 feet, so that the
climate is good. Brilliant, rushing mountain streams
tumble into Lake Abaya. There are pleasant pas-
tures and meadows for grazing land, but most of
the country is covered with forest, blackwood and

olive trees, coffee trees growing in the shade of the giant podocarpus. Coffee is native to Ethiopia and the name probably comes from the name of the Province of Kaffa, where the beans are especially rich.

The province was fairly new to the Empire. Half a century before Tafari arrived to take up his post as Governor, wild tribes in Sidamo ruled themselves, under their *balabats,* or chieftains. It had been a savage country. Now the young prince had come to register the land, to bring Imperial justice to the villages, to collect taxes due to him and to the central government in Addis Ababa. His position was somewhat like that of the governor of a territory of our own West during the early, lawless days of the American frontier. He traveled from village to village, riding his richly ornamented mule (for no horse could manage the crude mountain tracks), and with him rode a squadron of cavalry. Often the villagers were not inclined to respect the Governor's authority unless it was backed by the rifles of his troopers.

Court was held in the open air. Tafari sat on a ceremonial rug, a rich umbrella held over his head by a servant. Beside him stood another servant with a fly whisk to ward off bugs. He heard both sides of the case before him and then pronounced his sentence or announced his decision. There was no written law to be followed, only age-old tradition, some

of it going back to the days of King Solomon himself. Sometimes Tafari sought the advice of the
Elders, as was done in the days of the Old Testament. Sometimes he drew on what he had learned at
the Menelik School in Addis Ababa.

His task as Governor was twofold. Menelik expected him to make the Province produce its share
of grain, cattle, honey, and coffee, to add to the Imperial treasury. The more of these things that were
carried to Addis Ababa on mule trains, the more
Tafari would be praised by the Emperor and his
advisers. But in the back of Tafari's mind was the
vision of a new Ethiopia. As he rode through the
villages of Sidamo, little clusters of round houses
made of bamboo stalks, he was always ready to listen
when a villager ran up to his mule train, fell to his
knees with the cry of *"Abet! Abet!"*—"Hear my
grievance!"

In Sidamo the fierce tribesmen learned that they
would be listened to by the slim, aristocratic figure
on muleback, and that often after Tafari had heard
them, certain wrong things would be put right.

For eighteen months Lij Tafari ruled Sidamo in
the name of the Crown. It was his apprenticeship
and the place where he won his spurs. In a year and
a half he became known as one of the best provincial
governors in the Empire, a ruler who could be
trusted by the Emperor and the people alike.

Then one day, while he was holding court in a village above Lake Abaya, a messenger from Addis Ababa rode into the clearing where the villagers were assembled. He handed Tafari a scroll that bore the great seal of the Lion of Judah. Tafari read the Amharic words and his heart beat faster. For Menelik had appointed him Governor of Harar, his native province, great and powerful, and the land that his father had ruled until the day he died.

"Harar!" Tafari exclaimed. "I return to Harar!"

It was his birthright at last. Here in the grove of giant trees that covered the southern hillside, in his mind's eye there rose a vision of the walled city where he had lived as a boy. Sweet memories of his father's palace rushed into his mind. Then pain at the memory of his father.

"Harar!" his mind cried out again. "I return to Harar!"

He was sorry to leave Sidamo, for he had come to love the wild hill people and their country, but he knew that in Harar his real life's work would begin. Harar was great, and from Harar led the road to the throne room in Addis Ababa. There was the Queen, it was true. She was ruthless and she wanted to rule, to become the modern Queen of Sheba. There was Lij Yasu and Yasu's father, Ras Mikael. They were dangerous.

But there was the throne room in Addis Ababa, where sat the ailing Menelik. From that room the

Empire was ruled, and at eighteen, under the tall trees of the forests of Sidamo, Tafari felt in his bones that his own destiny, however it was to be played out, was in the end to lead to the throne.

He handed over control of Sidamo and traveled to Addis Ababa, to take his orders from Menelik before proceeding to Harar. When he entered the throne room, Tafari was shocked by Menelik's appearance. Fo many years Menelik had been the greatest soldier in Ethiopia, the tower of strength. It was a crushing blow for Tafari to see him as he was now—wasted and weakened by the effect of two massive brain hemorrhages, leaning heavily for support on the arm of one of his aides. It was not necessary to be a doctor to realize that the great King did not have many years to live. However, his mind, which had failed after each of the strokes, was now completely recovered, and so was the power of speech. When he spoke to Tafari, his voice was firm.

"I send you to Harar to take up where your father left off," the ailing Emperor told Tafari. "He was a great man. When you govern Harar, be guided by his memory, and you will govern well."

Tafari needed no reminder, for the memory of Ras Makonnen burned in his mind. He went back to his father's palace, inside the medieval walls of Harar. Everywhere, as he passed through the narrow, ancient streets, he was greeted with respect and love, for Ras Makonnen was a legend in Harar, almost a demigod. He had brought peace and prosperity to the old province and order to the old city. The people of Harar trusted Tafari to follow in the steps of his father, who had at his death been bent to the task of making Harar a model province.

"This is the key to our country's future," Tafari told his advisers. "If we can make Harar a good place to live, other provinces will follow us."

This concept of "model provinces" was to be at the heart of Tafari's program for the nation, when at last he became the Emperor. He knew that a country like Ethiopia, which was buried in the past, an Old Testament country, where the costumes and customs and crude tribal life, even the flat, unleavened bread, would not have seemed strange to King Solomon or King David—such a nation could not all at once be turned into a modern state. It must be done one step at a time, one province at a time, and the people must be led by the hand, out of the darkness of the past into the daylight of the future.

It was here in Harar, his native place, that Tafari meant to point the way to the future. He threw himself into the work of ruling a large province.

Meantime, he was a young man. At nineteen, as an important figure in the government, it was time for him to marry. And he was in love, madly in love. She was Waizero (Lady) Menen, the cousin of his rival, Lij Yasu, a delicate, olive-skinned girl, one of the most beautiful young women in attendance at Menelik's court, which was where Tafari had first seen her, on his return from Sidamo. She wore a felt hat with a pink silk ribbon, a violet collar, and a black silk coat, and she moved with the particular grace of well-born Amhara women.

In Ethiopia there are three forms of marriage. One is simply an arrangement which can be broken at any time and which in many countries might not be considered marriage at all. The second is a civil ceremony, with a property contract, from which divorce is easy. The third is a formal union, with all the pomp of the Coptic Church, and this is binding for life. It was the third form of marriage that was chosen by Tafari and Waizero Menen. Wearing gold crowns and gold mantles, they were married in the great stone church at Harar that had been built by Ras Makonnen. As they stood beneath the canopies in Ras Makonnen's church, while the priests chanted and the vows were offered, no one, except perhaps Tafari himself, knew that the pretty, shy young bride would one day be the Empress of Ethiopia.

It was a marriage that was to survive the years, through good times and bad, through war and peace, to prove a source of strength to Tafari in his struggles and a source of inspiration to the whole country; indeed, for a time, to the whole of the civilized world.

Tafari and his young bride lived at peace in Harar while Tafari went about his work of creating a model province. They were much in love and they were happy. Their life at home in Ras Makonnen's palace was a tender contrast to the hard, grinding work of administering a great province with an area larger than that of Belgium and Holland together, and a population of many millions of people.

In Addis Ababa, meanwhile, clouds were gathering at the Imperial court which were not encouraging for the future of the Empire. Menelik had a third stroke, and a fourth. At times he was helpless and had to be attended like a baby. At other times he regained his powers, became alert, and then desperately tried to make up for the time lost while he had been ill.

In this state of health, half sick and dazed much of the time, he was easy prey to his Empress, Queen Taitu. She has been compared to Lady Macbeth— ruthless, cruel, and ambitious. Above all, ambitious. She loved power for its own sake. She knew that in his heart of hearts the sick and aging Menelik wanted to appoint as his successor the son of his comrade Ras Makonnen, but Taitu was determined at any cost to prevent Tafari from becoming King.

"Lij Yasu is your grandson," she said to Menelik again and again. "He has a right to the throne."

"He is a waster," Menelik argued. "He is only a

boy, scarcely more than a child, but already he drinks *tej* and chases the pretty Galla girls."

Behind Menelik's back, Queen Taitu smiled. Systematically, she had corrupted the young Lij Yasu, until now he was in her power. "He is your grandson," she repeated. "He must succeed you on the throne."

At last the sick Emperor agreed.

"Very well, Lij Yasu shall be King of Kings when I die," he said. "But Ras Tasamma shall act as Regent until Lij Yasu is old enough to come to his senses. And I hope that age will be enough to bring that boy to his senses."

The idea of having a Prince Regent to make the actual decisions was sound enough. It is a practice followed in many countries, when the king is ill or insane or too young to rule. But Ras Tasamma was one of the Emperor Menelik's mistakes. He had been a brave soldier, and Menelik was apt to over-look other faults if a man was brave. Ras Tasamma was weak and corrupt; quickly, he became the tool of Queen Taitu.

After another stroke, Menelik became helpless forever, and it was Taitu who really ruled, through Ras Tasamma, until suddenly, in 1911, Ras Tasamma was taken ill and died.

The country was in grave danger. Before Menelik, the Emperor of Ethiopia had been a figurehead. The country was ruled, or rather misruled, by the various local princes, each Ras serving as his own master, looting the various provinces. There had been no unity, no central power. Menelik had changed all that, making the Rases responsible to the central power of the King of Kings. Now he lay paralyzed and unable to utter a word. The powerful Rases saw their chance to regain the strength they had lost. The affairs of the nation fell into confusion.

Beyond the borders of Ethiopia, others watched hungrily as the ancient Empire became more and more disorganized. In Rome, the Italian Foreign Office made plans for possible invasion. Italy already controlled the old Ethiopian seacoast province of Eritrea, and Italians still remembered the humiliating defeat inflicted upon their army by Menelik at Adowa. To the north was the Anglo-Egyptian Sudan, ruled from London and governed by British officers. In quiet offices in Whitehall in London, men of the British Colonial Office made plans involving Ethiopia's northern provinces, the land where the Blue Nile rises at Lake Tsana. The French controlled the Somali Coast, on the Red Sea. With the new railroad line, which ran from the French Somali port of Jibuti, there were men in Paris who saw the chance to add another sphere of influence to the already great French power in Africa.

For the first time since Adowa, the ancient Empire, the last truly independent nation in Africa, was in danger of falling under control of the colonial powers in Europe, which had already gobbled up all the rest of the Dark Continent, so that nowhere, except in Addis Ababa and in tiny Liberia, did black men rule in their own world.

The fate of the nation was at stake, but the Rases did not think of the welfare of the nation. Each one thought of his own domain and of his own treasure chests, filled with jewels and heavy silver Maria Theresa talers. They wanted a free hand.

When the Council of State, made up of the leading Rases, met in Addis Ababa after Ras Tasamma's death, they were expected to appoint a new Prince Regent. Instead, they looked at the half-drunken boy who had been named heir to the throne by his grandfather.

"When he can drink *tej* like a man, why does he need a Regent?" one of the tough old chieftains demanded.

"He is a man in other ways," said a second Ras.

"Let Lij Yasu himself be Regent," said a third.

And when the Rases cast their votes, it was Lij Yasu who became Regent, to act for the powerless Menelik. Again Queen Taitu smiled. She knew how to keep the headstrong prince under her control.

Lij Yasu had other ideas. When the power was his, he intended to use it.

It would be difficult to make a list of all the crimes that were committed by Lij Yasu during the years he held power. He had been a drunkard at thirteen, and other corruptions had followed. He loved cruelty for its own sake. He loved to watch while his troopers tortured an innocent Galla boy or girl. He was arrogant and dissolute, caring for nothing but his own pleasures, and these almost always involved inflicting pain on his most humble subjects.

Lij Tafari was concerned for Harar. Lij Yasu confirmed him as Governor, but he asked in return that Tafari swear an oath of loyalty to him. Because he loved his native province, Tafari accepted his cousin's terms and swore an oath of loyalty to the new Prince Regent.

From his post in Harar, Tafari watched what was happening to his country. His sense of loyalty was strong. Menelik was his ruler and Menelik, for whatever reason, had chosen Lij Yasu to be his heir. Tafari had given his word to Lij Yasu in good faith. So long as it remained humanly possible, Tafari would not do anything to interfere with Lij Yasu's rights, much as he might regret the excesses committed by his cousin.

And they were many.

Lij Yasu and his cavalry roamed the Danakil Desert, where Lij Yasu shot lions and enslaved thousands of Danakil and Somali tribesmen. Men were sold for eighty dollars. Virgin girls brought one hundred dollars. Children were sold for thirty dollars each. On one such expedition, when the villagers heard that Lij Yasu and his army were approaching, the people ran to hide in the mountains. In revenge, Lij Yasu's troopers, using their curved, broad-bladed swords, murdered three thousand men, women, and children.

"He simply likes the sight of blood," reported the British representative in Addis Ababa, when he described Lij Yasu's activities to his superiors in London.

Still the British supported Lij Yasu, in spite of his bloodthirsty nature, for Lij Yasu could be counted upon to play the game of the colonial powers. The British, French, and Italians were by this time engaged in a contest with the Turks and the Germans over control of the riches of Ethiopia. The rest of Africa, from the rich Mediterranean coastline, where the French held proud Algiers, to the Cape of Good Hope and Table Bay, where the Boers and the British held South Africa, was all in the hands of the white man. Ethiopia was the last piece of ripe African fruit to be picked by the white imperialists. If Lij Yasu served their purpose and gave them concessions, the men in London, Paris, Rome, and Berlin did not care how many Galla maidens were outraged or how many strong young Danakils were driven through the mountains to slavery. Over the teacups in London and across the wineglasses in Paris, they might murmur, "Oh, shocking!" or *"Mon Dieu, les sauvages!"* but at heart they cared for nothing except the chance to rob Ethiopia of her riches.

It was the old colonial story, the last of the African cards to be played, and to the white men in Europe, Lij Yasu seemed to be the perfect puppet, so they offered him money and looked away while the people of Ethiopia suffered.

5

To the rescue of his country

Toward the end of the year 1913, the Emperor
Menelik recovered from the dark agony of his illness long enough to realize that Ethiopia was being
ruined by a reckless, savage boy. His life work was
being destroyed, but he was too weak to take action
against Lij Yasu, who was ranging the hills with his
cavalry, gathering herds of slaves and driving them
to the slave markets. And Yasu was making deals
with the Mohammedan chieftains who controlled

the southern tribes. Even the Old Ethiopian Church was in danger.

Menelik stared through a window of the palace at Addis Ababa and sadly shook his head. It was hopeless. He did not have the strength to take command and put things right. His heart was broken, as well as his body. He turned to his attendants.

"Send to Athens," he said. "I am dying."

Two priests arrived from the Greek capital, bringing with them a container of Holy Water drawn from a spring on Mount Athos. Menelik's face and forehead were bathed with the sanctified water. The holy men murmured the last rites, then made the sign of the cross over the old man's rotting body.

"God help my people!" Menelik exclaimed.

Then he burst into tears and died.

Did he, in his last moments, foresee Tafari's victory over Lij Yasu? We do not know. We can only hope that the brave old warrior had this flash of hope at the end, a foreknowledge that Tafari would save the country.

In the palace, the Council of State gathered after Menelik's death. Things were going well for the Rases; they did not want to see any changes.

"We cannot let the people know," they decided. "If the news of Menelik's death spreads through the city and then to the outlying provinces, there will be civil war from one end of the country to the other."

So Menelik's death was concealed from the people. A *likamaquas,* or double, dressed in Menelik's clothes, occasionally appeared at a palace window in order to fool the crowds.

Lij Yasu returned to Addis Ababa, where he immediately ordered an enormous banquet that lasted for several days. He drank *tej* with his henchmen and feasted on strips of raw meat. Though Menelik's body was scarcely cold, Lij Yasu and his henchmen held a rowdy celebration. Then Yasu's father, Ras Mikael, arrived at the palace. In all of Ethiopia, only Ras Mikael had any control whatsoever over the mad Prince Regent.

"Leave things to me," he advised his son. "With Menelik dead, nothing is certain. Every Ras in the Empire will try to steal your place."

Ras Mikael went to the Cathedral, but the Archbishop flatly refused to cooperate, for he had heard the stories of Lij Yasu's dealings with the Mohammedan chiefs.

"I will not crown your son until he is twenty," the Archbishop said sternly. "And then only if he has learned to behave himself and proved that he is a good Christian."

But Ras Mikael was a clever politician. He spread the rumor that Lij Yasu was to be crowned in

October, 1914. From all over the Empire, the relatives of Menelik poured into Addis Ababa to hold a conference concerning the coronation. Tafari came with the others, but he had friends in the capital who warned him of danger. All of the other princes who might have been rivals to Lij Yasu were arrested and put into golden chains. Lij Yasu would have had them killed, except that Ethiopian law and custom forbids the execution of a royal prince.

Of all those who answered the summons, only Tafari escaped from the city, riding out into the night with his armed horsemen beside him. By the time Ras Mikael and Lij Yasu learned that he was gone, Tafari was far away in the mountains, on the way to Harar.

Once at home, on familiar ground, Tafari concentrated on his work in Harar, trying to ignore the turmoil into which Lij Yasu had plunged the country. At Addis Ababa the Prince Regent passed his nights in debauchery and remained in his bed until noontime, while his chiefs and advisers waited. The Turks were building strength with the tribesmen, and the Rases were robbing the people. Tafari knew that in the end Lij Yasu must be removed, but he felt that the time was not ripe. Besides, he had sworn an oath of loyalty and Tafari was not the man to break lightly a solemn oath.

Meanwhile, in the autumn of 1914, the Great

War in Europe had begun. The Turks were allies of
the Germans. Turkish agents in Addis Ababa
worked on Lij Yasu, for they felt that if he could
be won over and Ethiopia used as a base, all of British and French Africa might be conquered and the
old Turkish Empire restored.

With the help of the Turks, Lij Yasu was preparing his own ruin. He was meeting with the Mo-
hammedans, hinting that he intended to turn against
the established church of Ethiopia and make Ethiopia, one of the oldest Christian countries in the
world, into a Moslem state. He went to Dire Dawa,
a city on the railway line to the Red Sea coast, and
attended services in the mosque, praying as a
Moslem. Secret agents of the Turkish government
had introduced Lij Yasu to the use of hashish, a
powerful drug that he soon came to prefer to wine
and *tej*. Under the influence of hashish, he once announced that he was a descendant of the Prophet
Mohammed. To the Turkish Consul-General at
Harar, in Tafari's back yard, Lij Yasu presented an
Ethiopian flag upon which was embroidered, instead
of the Lion of Judah, a Turkish crescent and the
words: "There is no God but Allah."

Drunk with hashish and dreams of grandeur, Lij
Yasu was easily flattered into believing that he was
the new Mahdi, or Saviour, upon whose arrival the
Ethiopian Moslems waited. In his dreams, encouraged by the Turkish agents, he saw himself as ruler

not only of Ethiopia but of the Sudan and the Somaliland, perhaps even of Egypt, head of a great Moslem empire. He was persuaded that he was descended on his father's side from Fatima, daughter of the Prophet Mohammed.

There was no end to his madness and no end to the ruin he was bringing on the country. In the churches, Coptic priests offered up a prayer each day: "Since we can do nothing, may God kill him soon!"

Only one man was strong enough to oppose Lij Yasu, and that was Tafari. Lij Yasu was determined to get rid of his rival.

On Lake Aramayo, a broad, deep lake surrounded by dense forests, cool and peaceful, Tafari kept a small boat. When he had the time he liked to sail on the calm waters of Aramayo with his friend Ras Imru and his old tutor Aba Samuel. One afternoon, far from shore, the little boat sprang a leak and sank. Tafari was saved, but the Aba Samuel was drowned.

"It was no accident," Tafari was told.

At first Tafari refused to believe that Yasu would stoop to the murder of his own cousin, but later a Moslem servant confessed that he had made a hole in the boat and filled it with mud, which had dissolved and fallen out into the water. It had been an effort to murder Tafari, and behind the plot were Lij Yasu and his Turkish friends.

Tafari went down to the shore of the lake and stared out across the calm waters.

"The time has come," he said, speaking to the deep forest silence. "Yasu must go. Now everything depends upon the Council of Ministers."

6

The seizure of power

In Addis Ababa, the Council of Ministers was under pressure from the Church, which feared that Lij Yasu would make the country Mohammedan, and from the British, French, and Italian officials, who saw that the Turks and Germans might take over, with Lij Yasu as a puppet chieftain.

The Council of Ministers made excuses, stalling for time. They put off the priests and the Allied legations with promises that somehow they would make

Lij Yasu behave. They were afraid of Lij Yasu's hard-riding cavalry and more interested in making money than in the welfare of the country.

They argued for days. Then, at last, a plan was proposed that seemed to offer a way out. In the monastery at Entoto, in seclusion, lived the Princess Zauditu (or Judith), a daughter of Menelik by an earlier marriage. She had been the wife of Ras Gugsa, a powerful prince, but was now living apart from her husband.

"Let Zauditu be made Empress," it was suggested. "And let Tafari be appointed Regent, with the right to succeed her."

The Rases agreed and sent for Tafari. He came willingly, though he knew that when he left Harar, his life was in danger from Yasu and from the Turkish agents. And his young wife, Waizero Menen, was pregnant for the second time. She had given birth to a daughter; this time she and Tafari hoped that the child would be a son. She could not go to Addis Ababa with Tafari because of her condition, and he wanted to be sure that she would be protected. He sent for his good friend, Major Dodds, the British Consul at Harar.

"Promise me that you will look after my wife," he asked the major. The promise was given, and Tafari transferred money to a bank in England so that if he should be murdered by Lij Yasu's men

his wife and children would be cared for. These
things arranged, Tafari set out for the capital.

Soon after he arrived, a courier came from Harar
with the news that Waizero Menen's child had been
born. It was the son they had wanted. Tafari asked
for permission to leave the city. He was refused.
Secretly, he arranged with Major Dodds and other
trusted friends in Harar to have his wife and children smuggled out of the city. Waizero Menen escaped from Harar without a moment to spare. A
few hours after she departed, a squadron of Lij
Yasu's horsemen surrounded Tafari's house. At the
same time, Lij Yasu announced that Tafari had
been removed as Governor of Harar.

When he heard this news, Tafari smiled. His
oath to Lij Yasu was no longer valid and he could
proceed with a clear conscience. In Addis Ababa,
he waited with his own bodyguard, a loaded re-
volver strapped to his waist.

"If they come for me, they will find me waiting
with a gun," he told the British ambassador.

For Tafari, a man of peace, these were violent
words.

Rumors spread through the capital. Shots were
fired in the streets. Restless soldiers wandered
through the city, carrying rifles, not knowing where
their orders would be coming from. In the foreign
missions, British, French, Germans, and Turks pre-

pared for any emergency, even the total collapse of all government in Ethiopia. In the ministries, clerks were burning official papers and the telegraph lines to Europe hummed with messages asking for instructions. There were rumors of revolution and rumors that foreign armies were marching toward the Ethiopian frontiers.

The rumors reached Lij Yasu and he panicked. With an escort of Mohammedan horsemen armed with long, ornamented rifles, he rode through the gates of Addis Ababa toward Dire Dawa, on the railway line to French Somaliland. In Dire Dawa he went at once to the Mosque and prayed to Allah. He was among his Moslem allies and for the moment he felt safe.

In Addis Ababa, the Council was called into session. Tafari had not been idle. He had the Church on his side and the Archbishop was prepared to excommunicate Lij Yasu, an action that would drive him from the Church and make him unfit to be Emperor. The Council was ready to remove Lij Yasu from the throne and make Zauditu Empress, with Tafari as Regent, but they wanted some assurance that their ancient feudal rights would not be tampered with too much. They insisted that the old soldier, Hapta Giorgis, be made Minister of War, to serve beside Tafari. In this way the Rases hoped to keep Tafari's modern ideas under some control.

In the great Council hall, the leaders of Ethiopia met. Tafari stood before them, Hapta Giorgis at his side. The Archbishop Mattheo, splendid in his robes and mitre, solemnly pronounced the words that cast Lij Yasu from the ancient Coptic Church.

"From this day forward, Oh Great men of Ethiopia," he said, "you are freed from your oath to Lij Yasu. We will never submit to Islam."

In the yard of the Royal Palace, the royal drums throbbed out the news to the people. Artillery fired volleys in salute to the new Empress and the new Prince Regent. In the streets the simple people waited for the official proclamation. When it came, they rejoiced.

"Hear, Oh Christian people of Ethiopia: Our religion and our government were in danger. For the protection of our religion and our ancient government that goes back to the great King Solomon, the Council has appointed the Princess Zauditu to be Empress and Ras Tafari to be Regent and heir to the throne of the King of Kings. Because this has been done with the consent of all, go forth into the land and rejoice."

Through the streets of Addis Ababa, under a golden canopy, rode Zauditu, the new Empress of Ethiopia. The people cheered, but their eyes were fixed on the slight figure who rode at her side. Ras Tafari (he had been made Ras when he was appointed Regent) had grown the short, well-trimmed beard that he was to wear for the rest of his life. He was a figure of dignity and courage, the sad, poetic eyes filled with a sense of destiny that the crowds in the streets seemed to feel. For the first time since the death of Menelik, Ethiopia had a ruler worthy of the name. Tafari, they felt, was a man of peace and progress, a devout Christian, and a man of the future, willing to devote all his life to the welfare of his country.

Ethiopia had been saved, but the struggle was not quite over.

Zauditu was Empress and Ras Tafari was Regent, the true ruler of the country, but Lij Yasu was still in the hills with his horsemen, and as long as he remained at large, there was the threat of civil war. The large Moslem population was restless and there were Rases in the outlying provinces who resented Tafari's power. They would support Lij Yasu. But Yasu himself was not as dangerous as his father, Ras Mikael, a shrewd old war lord who knew how to fight. Certainly, Ras Mikael would not sit quietly by and watch the disgrace of his son. He was too proud for that.

What would Ras Mikael do? This was the question asked by the Council of State and by Tafari himself.

They did not have long to wait for an answer. The telegraph line that connected Addis Ababa with Europe passed through Dessye, capital of Ras

Mikael's territory. It was cut. Then Ras Mikael took to the field with his army.

Lij Yasu had fled to Harar, where there was a large Moslem community. He made desperate appeals to the British, asking for protection. He was refused. From Addis Ababa, Tafari ordered a column of troops under Ras Balcha to march on Harar, and he sent a message to the Governor of Harar, ordering him to arrest Lij Yasu and place him in chains. Another army, under Lul Seged, was sent north to the frontiers of Ras Mikael's kingdom to hold the old war lord in check.

In Harar, the Moslem chieftains appealed to Lij Yasu.

"You are one of the Faithful," they told the frightened Prince. "Proclaim a Holy War against Tafari. Every Moslem in Ethiopia will come to your support."

Had they been dealing with a brave man, the Moslem chiefs would have been a real threat to Tafari's rule. But Lij Yasu was a coward. He slipped through the main gate of Harar at night, deserting his Moslem retainers. Tafari's troops, under Ras Balcha, swarmed through the gates of Harar and cut down the Mohammedan rebels. The streets and alleyways of the old walled city were jammed with bodies and the stench of the rotting corpses could be smelled for miles around Harar. At night the gates were opened and troops of hyenas entered the town. Soon the streets and the alleys were cleared. Balcha's soldiers ruled Harar in the name of the new Prince Regent.

In the north, Ras Mikael moved his squadrons of fresh horsemen against Tafari's troops, who fought under Lul Seged. Seged's ponies were footsore and bleeding after the long trek north (Ethiopian horses were seldom shod). His men were exhausted, having had no rest during their forced march. Mikael trapped them in a narrow gorge and cut them down, his cavalry wielding their heavy sabers, his marksmen firing from the hillsides. It was a slaughter rather than a battle. Lul Seged was killed in action. Back to Addis Ababa trickled a few survivors, bringing news of defeat to Tafari.

"Ras Mikael is on the rampage," the British ambassador reported to London. "Unless Tafari moves at once, he is lost, and the country will fall into anarchy."

But Tafari knew Ethiopia better than the British. He understood that the real key to victory was in politics. He was working behind the scenes, persuading the important chieftains to support him. In the meantime, he sent Hapta Giorgis north with an army of ten thousand men.

"You must hold up Mikael at all costs," he said to the tough old Minister of War. "The fate of the country depends on your soldiers."

Through the narrow gorges, high mountains

towering toward the sky, Hapta Giorgis moved north with his army, taking up positions that blocked Mikael. The two old fighters faced each other, neither for the moment prepared to move.

When his arrangements in Addis Ababa were completed, Tafari himself rode north with a second army to join forces with Hapta Giogris at Sallale, on the pretty Sendaffa Plain, about fifty miles north of Addis Ababa, in the highlands of the Province of Shoa.

It was mid-November. After the heavy rains, the countryside was green and alive with flowers— daisies, lilies, African orchids. The tents of the armies, green, gold, red, and yellow, were like larger flowers in the rays of the flashing sun. The sky by day was like blue chalk, marked by a few fleecy clouds. The air was fresh as clear spring water. By night the campfires glittered like stars, picking out the lines of the encampments. The two armies waited for battle.

The grand strategy—to bottle up Ras Mikael —had been Tafari's. Now he decided to take command of the actual battle and to manage tactics as well. In his yellow breeches and silken shirt, an ornamented *kufta,* or battle helmet, on his head, he rode through the lines inspecting his troops, offering here and there a word of encouragement to the men. He was tense but confident. The stakes of the battle were great. If Ras Mikael could overcome

Tafari's forces, he could move on to Addis Ababa and restore Lij Yasu to the throne.

For several days the armies waited. Then before dawn one morning, Tafari's camp was aroused by the sounds of wild geese honking in the air, started up from their coverts. Mikael's army was on the move, intending to mount a surprise attack.

Tafari was ready for him, but the battle that followed was bloody. It was combat hand to hand, in the style of Pickett's charge and the awful battles of our own Civil War. For five hours the two armies charged and recharged across the plain of Sendaffa. The pretty, tropical flowers were trampled under the troopers' feet and the pretty Plain of Sendaffa was red with the troopers' blood. First the tide went one way, then the other, but as darkness fell and long shadows crossed the hillsides, Ras Mikael's army at last was beaten back. Mikael himself was surrounded by a troop of Tafari's cavalry.

"Surrender!" shouted one of Tafari's officers. "We will guarantee your safety. You have fought like a brave man."

There was a moment of pause in the battle. Then old Ras Mikael, his face smeared with blood, tears of rage coursing down his cheeks, uttered a curse and flung his shield to the ground. For a few seconds he held his sword in his hand, staring at the blade that had served him well. Then he tossed it away, uttering a cry of despair.

On his horse Tafari sat, looking over the field of battle. He had won. His regime was safe. But there was sadness in his heart as he looked on the dead and wounded men, his own countrymen all.

Four days after the Battle of Sendaffa, Tafari led a victory parade through the streets of Addis Ababa. Behind him, trotting on spirited horses, were his own Harar cavalry. Behind the army came the captives. There was Ras Mikael, chained at the wrists, neck, and ankles, but still defiant. Watching Mikael, Tafari said, "He is a brave man. He marches and looks like a king."

At the very end of the parade came the remnants of Lul Seged's army, which had been cut to pieces by Ras Mikael. There were a few dozen men, most of them wounded. The watching crowd was silent. Last of all came a boy of about seven. He wore nothing on his little body except a lion's skin, the lion's skin cape of a great warrior. It was the son of Lul Seged, marching in memory of his dead father.

7

Prince Regent

The battle against Ras Mikael's army had been won, but Lij Yasu remained at large, roaming through the Danakil deserts, his inflamed brain still filled with wild dreams of glory and a return to power. One day he prayed in a Mosque, the next in a Coptic church. Though the Moslem chiefs held him in contempt they hoped to use him, and so long as he was free he was a threat to Tafari.

There were other threats at home.

Tafari was known as a ruler who wanted to improve the condition of the common people, to free the slaves, and to bring Ethiopia into the modern world. Queen Zauditu was vain and stupid and thought only of her own comfort. The Council of State, made up as it was of Rases and chiefs, wanted to keep the old ways, because the old ways kept them powerful and rich. The people themselves had nothing to say. There was no voting, no constitution.

For a time Tafari was forced to be a kind of juggler, keeping the various forces in balance and unable to move forward as he desired. In the remote provinces, wild chiefs rose in civil war, fighting over this mountain or that one. Only the fact that all of Europe was engaged in a life and death struggle prevented Ethiopia from being seized as a colony by one or another of the European states, as had almost every other part of the so-called Dark Continent. The Moslem tribes were troublesome; Tafari was almost alone.

Toward the end of the war in Europe, Lij Yasu and a force of Mohammedan rebels were established in the fortress of Magdala, near Ras Mikael's old capital of Dessye. The fortress was on a mountain peak reached by steep, narrow trails, all of which were under the rifles of Lij Yasu's people on the battlements. Great cauldrons of water were kept boiling, ready to be thrown upon Tafari's troops if they dared to approach the fortress.

Tafari appealed to the British government for aircraft with which to bomb Magdala, pointing out that Lij Yasu was really an agent of the Turks, who were Great Britain's enemies. The British ambassador tried to persuade his government, but in the end Tafari was refused. He sent a force to besiege Magdala. They could see Lij Yasu himself on the battlements, madly dancing and laughing at them. Morale was low among Tafari's forces and the men were killing their mules for food. Still, they held the fortress in siege. In the end, Lij Yasu escaped, slipping through Tafari's lines in the night. He was on the loose again, gathering forces as he rode through the countryside. In Addis Ababa, the old war lords plotted against Tafari, afraid of losing their slaves and riches. The Empress Zauditu joined the plots against him. She had been in touch with her former husband, Ras Gugsa, and hoped somehow to bring him into power. Tafari's regency hung in the balance and so did the future of Ethiopia as an independent state.

With the aid of Turkish money, Lij Yasu had formed an army. While it existed, it was a threat to Tafari's power. In the end, old Hapta Giorgis turned the tide in Tafari's favor. Against a force of

40,000 Moslem cavalrymen and spearmen, the War Minister stood firm, using his artillery and machine guns with all the art of a modern commander. Although Lij Yasu's Mohammedan horsemen were fanatically brave, modern weapons prevailed against them. In the pitched battle on the plain before Dessye, 18,000 casualties lay on the bloody field of battle when at last Hapta Giorgis had won.

Lij Yasu escaped again, but he was finished. He tried to reach Arabia but failed. He was sick in mind and body, rotting to death in a Danakil village. Tafari refused to send a detachment to bring him in as a prisoner.

"He is no longer a danger," Tafari said. "Let him die out there and alone."

Tafari was too busy in Addis Ababa to bother any longer with Lij Yasu. He was reforming the government, putting an end to graft, bringing some efficiency into affairs. Some of his most dangerous enemies were thrown into the dungeons. And, on Mount Entoto, where she had been living in retirement, Menelik's widow, old Queen Taitu, died. Even in retirement, she had been one of Tafari's enemies, and her death, at seventy-six, was a relief.

Still Tafari was not in the clear. Blocking his efforts to reform the country were the Empress Zauditu, the war lords, and the Ministers of State. All of them knew that any improvement in the condition of the common people would mean loss of power for themselves. They lived like feudal lords and they were determined to preserve their privileges. Even the Church stood in his way.

Tafari nearly lost heart. In 1918, he fell victim to the savage flu epidemic that swept across Europe. For weeks he lay near death, his fever raging. His spirits sank and he yearned for the peace of his native province of Harar. In his illness there were moments when he expressed regret that he had ever left Harar.

"There is only one man who wishes his country well," wrote the British ambassador in his report to London. "That is the Regent, Tafari Makonnen. If he loses, the country will fall into anarchy. It may be necessary for the European powers to intervene in order to prevent utter chaos."

Tafari was weakened by illness, but his soul had been governed since childhood by two powerful forces: love of country and courage. He fought his way back to life, and after a few weeks at Harar, where he rested and regained his strength, he was ready to face the world again.

On the Western Front in Europe, the fighting had stopped after four long years of war. Germany and her Turkish ally had been defeated. On the day after Christmas in 1918, when the great powers were meeting at Versailles to plan the peace, Tafari wrote to King George V of England to tell him that all over Ethiopia, thanksgiving services for the Allied victory would be held in the Coptic churches.

Then he added: "We in Ethiopia wish to enter into closer relations with other nations. We intend shortly to send a special mission to Europe. We hope that our representatives will be favorably received by Your Majesty's Government."

A simple note, but important. When he wrote to the King of England, Tafari knew that he was breaking with the old Ethiopian tradition of isolation. He was opening the gate to the hated *ferengi,* the foreigners. He was also announcing to Ethiopia and to the world that he was in the saddle and that Tafari Makonnen was the true ruler of Ethiopia.

For two years, he walked slowly. Then, by a stroke of luck, the Danakil tribes grew tired of Lij Yasu. They sold him to the Empress Zauditu and he was turned over to Ras Kassa, war lord of the Tigre Province and a man trusted by Tafari. Bound, according to ancient custom, in chains of solid gold, he was imprisoned in a castle at Axum, ancient seat of Ethiopian kings. He was not mistreated. Medical attention was provided, and when he had partly recovered his health, Yasu was permitted to enjoy his favorite diversions. He lived in luxury and slept on a silken bed. He was attended by servants. But he was no longer of any importance in the affairs of the country.

Now Tafari was faced by three opponents: the Empress, Hapta Giorgis, the War Minister, and the Archbishop of the Ethiopian Church. The Empress was ambitious for herself and for her former husband, Ras Gugsa. Hapta Giorgis, though loyal to Tafari, wanted to keep the old ways of slavery and feudal power. The Archbishop was afraid that the power of the Church would be weakened by the reforms Tafari proposed, especially by the spread of education.

Ethiopia, in the nineteen-twenties, lay in the darkest ignorance. Less than one percent of the population could read and write. There were hundreds of thousands of slaves. Addis Ababa itself was a mud village, except for the few roads Tafari had built. There were no highways between the cities. There was one railway line, from Addis Ababa to Jibuti, on the coast of French Somaliland. There were no teachers, no engineers, no doctors. The army, though famous for the bravery of its soldiers, was badly organized and badly equipped. In the hill provinces, far from the capital, the Rases and the war lords ruled in the same way their ancestors had ruled two thousand years before, paying little or no attention to the young Prince Regent in Addis Ababa.

In spite of her backwardness, however, Tafari was determined that Ethiopia should become a member of the League of Nations, the world organization of states set up after the end of World War I, with the idea that world peace could be protected by international union. With the help of Italy and France, Tafari succeeded, and Ethiopia was elected a member of the League of Nations in 1924.

It was the first real step into the future. Now that Ethiopia was in the League, Tafari decided to make another break with tradition.

"I am going to Europe, to see the outside world for myself," he told his wife, Waizero Menen.

"What of the Empress?" he was asked. "She is still a danger."

"I will leave Hapta Giorgis to look after the Empress," replied Tafari.

"And Hapta Giorgis? He has ambitions."

"Ras Kassa will see that Hapta Giorgis behaves himself," answered Tafari with some confidence.

Such was the web of intrigue that infected the Imperial court. It was dangerous for Tafari to turn his back for an instant, but he decided to take the risk. He sailed from the French port of Jibuti with Waizero Menen, Ras Seyoum, and Ras Hailu. Thirty attendants were in his party. In cages, in the hold of the ship, were six lions: two as presents for the King of England, two for the Paris Zoo, and two for the President of France. He also brought with him a Processional Cross to be placed in the nave of Westminster Abbey, one of the holiest places in England. Tafari wished to remind the Brit-

ish that his country was one of the very oldest of
Christian nations.

As he rode in state through the streets of London
in a glittering royal Rolls-Royce, Tafari's thoughts
must have turned to compare the majesty of the
British capital with his own Addis Ababa. Of all
cities, surely London is the most imperial, and Tafari
felt the sense of power. He traveled to Oxford and
looked at the towers and spires of the great university, and to Cambridge, where he stood on the silent
banks of the Cam and drank in the beauty of the
ancient Cambridge colleges. His heart burned for his
own country.

"We must have schools," he said softly in the
quiet Cambridge evening. "A university."

In London, the British government presented to
Tafari the crown of old Emperor Theodore, which
had been captured from Ethiopia by a British puni-
tive force under General Napier.

He did not get much more than Theodore's old
crown. He had wanted a free port in Jibuti, for
Ethiopia had no outlet to the sea. He did not get it.
He wanted financial aid for internal development.
He got promises and encouragement, but no
money. In Rome, at the Palazzo Venezia, he sat
across the table from the man who was, a few years
later, to become the greatest enemy in the history
of Ethiopia. This was Benito Mussolini—"Il Duce"
—dictator of Italy.

"We will help you. Do not worry," Mussolini said to Tafari. "Depend upon us. Italy is your friend."

How good a friend, Tafari was to learn and on the bloody field of battle, while the world stood by and watched. But that was in the future. Back in Addis Ababa after his trip abroad, Tafari looked at his country with new eyes and a mind that had been changed by the sights and sounds of the great capitals of Europe . . . London, Paris, Rome. He had known that Ethiopia was backward; now he realized that she was centuries behind.

"We must build roads, schools, hospitals," he said to the Empress Zauditu and to Hapta Giorgis, as well as to the Archbishop.

They opposed him, they tried to block his way, but Tafari went forward. In Europe he had bought a motor car. Painted with the red, green, and yellow colors of Ethiopia, this car became a familiar sight to the people of Addis Ababa as the Prince Regent personally drove out to lay the first stones of new sections of roadway being built to replace the rutted mule tracks that served the city as streets. He founded a school, in spite of the opposition of the Rases and the Archbishop.

"The crying need is for education," he told the sullen Rases, most of whom could neither read nor write. "Without an educated class we cannot maintain our independence, let alone go forward. I have built this school as a beginning. I appeal to wealthy people to follow my example."

The Tafari Makonnen School, the first the Prince Regent founded, had places for 180 boys. Together with the Menelik School, which Tafari himself had attended, this brought the grand total of school places in the entire country to 291—a feeble beginning for a man who hoped to lead the nation out of darkness, but a beginning nevertheless.

The Empress had sneered at Tafari when he took Ethiopia into the League of Nations. The Rases had grumbled. "Now we are under the eyes of the foreigners," they had said.

In 1925, they were to realize that Tafari had been wise.

The great colonial powers of Europe had welcomed Tafari as a Royal Prince and pretended to respect the rights of his country, when he had traveled in Europe. Later, they were not so pleasant. Without bothering to consult the Ethiopian government, the British and the Italians together decided to build a dam at Lake Tsana, the enormous inland sea that feeds the Blue Nile, a river that flows through the Sudan, joining the White Nile and flowing on through Egypt.

When Tafari heard of these plans for a dam at Lake Tsana, he was furious.

"They will learn that they are not dealing with savages or with colonial subjects," he said. "They are dealing with a sovereign power and a full member of the League of Nations."

To the League Tafari addressed a note, protesting the action of the British and the Italians."

"Throughout our history," he wrote, "we have seldom met with foreigners who did not desire to possess Abyssinian territory and to destroy our independence. With God's help and thanks to the courage of our soldiers, we have always, come what might, stood proud and free in our native mountains."

The British and Italians backed down. With the League of Nations behind him, Tafari had asserted the right of a poor and underdeveloped nation, and he had carried off the protest. Lake Tsana remained in Ethiopian hands.

"We have won this time," Tafari told the Empress. "But we must put our house in order. It is bad enough to be ignorant, but it is wicked that some of our Rases should be proud to be ignorant. We even have some who think it is right to make slaves of our people."

"We have always had slavery," the Empress protested.

"It must stop," Tafari insisted. He looked the Empress straight in the eye. She and Hapta Giorgis both bought and sold slaves and held slaves on their estates. Every rich household in Ethiopia was served by slaves. Even modest farmers in the green uplands were apt to own a slave or two.

"While I live, I shall have slaves," the Empress said defiantly. "You go too fast with your new ideas. The old ways have been good to us."

Tafari bowed. All of his life, one of his great virtues had been patience. He had learned how to wait. And he had an advantage. He was young. His opponents were old. Time was working on the side of progress.

The first of his opponents to go was the old war lord Hapta Giorgis. Though he had respected the old soldier and perhaps even loved him, Tafari had no time for sentiment. Before the Empress could digest the news of the War Minister's death, Tafari moved his own soldiers into Hapta Giorgis's domain. The slaves were freed. The great caskets of gold and silver were divided among Tafari's allies. And the Ethiopian Army passed under the control of Tafari. In her palace at Addis Ababa, the Empress bit her lip in anger, but there was nothing she could do. Tafari had moved too swiftly.

Later in the same year Abuna Mattheos, Archbishop of the Ethiopian Church, died at the age of eighty-three. The Archbishop had opposed Tafari's reforms, not because he wanted to make himself rich, like the reactionary Rases, but because he was afraid that progress would weaken the hold of the Church on the people. But he had fought Tafari nevertheless, and now he was dead. A new Archbishop would be sent out from Cairo, headquarters of the Coptic Church. Tafari had always believed that the Ethiopian Church should be headed by an Ethiopian Archbishop, but this was no time to oppose ancient customs. He did insist, however, that the new Archbishop be a man with modern ideas, ideas that would match his own.

As he marched in the long procession that followed the old Archbishop's body through the streets of Addis Ababa, Tafari brooded about the future. Now, he thought, only the Empress stood between him and the reforms he had planned for the country. And Zauditu, by herself, was no match for Tafari Makonnen.

8

The palace revolt

The Empress Zauditu was not quite willing to step into the background without a last effort to gain power. Secretly, she met with the ministers of state who thought that Tafari was going too fast and too far with his reforms. Together, the Empress and the ministers planned to get rid of Tafari by force. They bribed members of the Imperial Guard; some of the Rases brought in their own soldiers.

Was Tafari aware of the plot that was being

hatched behind his back? We do not know for certain, but the calmness he showed would indicate that he felt no fear, and inside the palace he had a network of loyal people who may have informed him of the planned revolt.

On a morning in 1928, Tafari went down from his own house, the "Little Gebbi" to the royal palace, or "Big Gebbi." As soon as he was inside the palace the gates were closed by the plotters. Machine guns had been mounted on the roofs of buildings that commanded the palace. Inside the palace, the Empress Zauditu challenged Tafari.

"You are trying to assume all power," she said. "I am the Empress. You are trying to push me aside."

"Your Imperial Majesty is mistaken," Tafari said coldly. "I am trying to save my country."

His own troops were some distance away. He was alone, but unafraid. Contemptuously, he faced the soldiers of the Palace Guard, whose rifles were raised. It was a contest of wills, and Tafari won. Under his cool, fearless gaze, the rifles were lowered. Somehow, the soldiers understood where the real power lay.

"Open the gates," Tafari commanded.

The palace gates were thrown open. Tafari walked calmly into the courtyard, his back to the rifles of the guards. He mounted his mule and rode away toward his own house. Against the armed soldiers of the Empress he had won the day simply by keeping his temper and refusing to display a trace of fear. The palace soldiers watched the slim figure in his dark red cape, riding away with his mule at a walk, as though nothing whatever had happened.

That night Tafari's troops moved into the palace yard and arrested the Imperial Guard and its commander. Tafari entered the palace and spoke to the Empress in sharp, brisk terms. He left no doubt in her mind that he was the ruler of Ethiopia and that she was a figurehead.

The following day the Council of Ministers met in the hall of the Old Palace. They realized that their only hope was to cooperate with Tafari.

"He is the man of the future," the wiser heads agreed.

The Council asked the Empress to create Tafari a Negus, or King. It would not add to his power as Regent, but it would give him greater prestige. It was a petition that had the force of a command. With a trembling hand, the angry Empress signed the parchment that gave Tafari the title of King. As she signed the document, she knew in her heart that the struggle with Tafari was over and that she had lost. The old Ethiopia of slavery and ignorance was doomed. The road to the future would be the one planned by Tafari.

The ceremony that made Tafari a King took

place at dawn on a cool September morning. An enormous silk canopy had been erected in the courtyard of the palace. Behind it rose the stone mass of the old Church of the Trinity. There was a gilded throne for the Empress and another for Tafari. Members of the diplomatic corps were present in their glittering uniforms. The Itchege, or Chief of the Monks, blessed the Empress and Tafari. Then Tafari walked slowly forward and knelt before the throne of the Empress. Servants held silk curtains around Tafari and Zauditu as the crown of a Negus was placed upon Tafari's head. The silken curtains fell away Tafari's officers drew their swords and raised them in salute, forming an arch of glittering steel. Then his soldiers rushed forward and carried Tafari on their shoulders to the Church of the Trinity. Alone in the rays of the morning sun, under the bright silk tent, stood the Empress of Ethiopia, a lonely and forgotten figure. In an open carriage, wearing the crown of a Negus, Tafari rode back to his palace, bowing to the crowds that lined the way.

Now he was King as well as Regent, and he had the Council of State behind him. He moved with caution, but he moved. The country needed, first of all, roads. And to understand the difficulty of providing roads in Ethiopia, you must imagine a country that is a succession of deep gorges, one after the other. Great bridges and viaducts were needed;

the roadway itself often had to be carved out of solid rock. It was a task to challenge the world's greatest engineers. Money, men, and machinery were required, and to get these, Tafari knew that Ethiopia must trade with Europe. The Rases were afraid that to open up the country to trade would bring the curse of colonialism—the curse that had blighted all of Africa, by means of which the powerful white man turned the weaker black man into a victim, another kind of a slave.

Tafari knew that he took a risk, but he decided the risk must be taken. He trusted himself and his people to preserve the nation's independence, which went back to the days before the Birth of Christ.

But first he must deal with the Church. Many of the priests were backward, but the new Abuna, or Archbishop, sent out from Cairo, was a reasonable man. "The Church must concern itself with spiritual matters," Tafari told Archbishop Kyril. "Politics are my affair."

The Archbishop Kyril agreed. He also agreed to appoint five new Bishops from Ethiopia—a break with the past—and he said to Tafari, "I shall be happy to receive the names of the priests to be appointed from your majesty." So for the first time in history the Ethiopian Church—daughter of the Coptic Church in Egypt—had a measure of independence.

Tafari's first act as King was to sign an agreement with Mussolini, the Italian dictator, permitting trade and guaranteeing Ethiopia's safety. He awarded the alcohol monopoly to a group of Belgian distillers, though they were not permitted to manufacture *tej* and *talla,* the two local drinks. In his native province of Harar, Tafari offered cotton monopolies to French and Belgian firms, with the idea of competing with the famous cotton from Egypt. He leased coffee plantations to the Belgians. An oil-pressing monopoly was arranged with the Greeks. Swiss and Italian concerns began to cut timber on the mountain slopes outside the capital.

Soon Addis Ababa was swarming with foreign engineers and businessmen. The Rases looked on them with suspicion. They were *ferengi,* hated foreigners, but Tafari knew that they were needed.

He tried to put the country's money on a sound basis. In some places, salt blocks were still used as a means of exchange. The only currency recognized by most Ethiopians was the Maria Theresa talers, a silver coin the size and weight of the American silver dollar or the British crown. Talers were heavy to carry and inconvenient, but many years were to pass before the people would accept the paper money issued by the Bank of Abyssinia, which had been chartered by Menelik.

With money coming into the country from the foreign concessions, Tafari modernized the army. He was not a soldier by instinct, but he knew that a disciplined force was needed for the safety of the state. The Belgians sent trained officers, and Tafari's soldiers were provided with modern weapons: rifles, machine guns, light tanks, efficient mountain artillery. But his infantry, as in ages past, continued to march on bare feet. Smartly uniformed from head to ankles, they could not be persuaded to wear shoes.

From Kenya, the British colony to the south, Tafari brought back Ethiopians who had served in the King's African Rifles, smart soldiers, trained to British spit and polish and to British precision drill. These men became his officers and noncommissioned officers. He encouraged freed slaves to join the ranks.

From the French he bought four modern aircraft. They were armed with machine guns and carried small bombs. He hired two French pilots, daring types who looped and sideslipped in true French fashion between the peaks of the Entoto Mountains.

In Rome, Mussolini frowned at the speed with which Tafari was bringing progress to his country. The Italians wanted a king they could control, not a strong, independent monarch. How could Tafari be checked or even removed from power? That was the question Mussolini asked his advisers in Fascist Rome.

At last Mussolini hit on a plan. In the north of

Ethiopia, there was one Ras who had refused to follow Tafari's lead. This was Ras Gugsa, who had once been the husband of the Empress Zauditu. Secretly, the Italians encouraged Ras Gugsa to make a revolution against Tafari. Breaking their agreement with Tafari, the Italians supplied Ras Gugsa with rifles and with hundreds of thousands of rounds of ammunition.

Meanwhile, Ras Gugsa made his plans, perhaps with the help of advisers from Italy. He spread rumors throughout the north that Tafari was secretly a Roman Catholic, that he was in league with the French Jesuits. "Did he not defy the Archbishop when he opened his school and staffed it with French priests?" Ras Gugsa demanded. "He has opened the country to the French and the Belgians, Roman Catholics all of them."

The rumors spread that Tafari intended to convert Ethiopia to Rome by force. From the northern hillsides, tribesmen rallied to the banners of Ras Gugsa. And in her isolated chambers in the palace at Addis Ababa, the Empress Zauditu's pulse must have quickened when she received a secret message from her ex-husband, telling her of his plans to restore her to power, with himself as Prince Consort.

In the spring of 1930, Ras Gugsa rode out from the north at the head of an army of 35,000 men, all of them filled with religious zeal inspired by the lies Ras Gugsa had spread, new rifles on their shoulders, their belts filled with Italian bullets. They camped on the flat Plain of Anchim, the officers' tents blooming like brightly colored flags, the men squatting around their fires, swallowing *tej* and raw meat. Suddenly there was a terrible sound in the sky overhead. The tribesmen looked up to see Tafari's aircraft, flying wing-tip to wing-tip. From the sky came thousands of leaflets, warning the tribesmen that unless they broke camp and went home, the planes would return and drop death instead of leaflets.

On the morning of March 31, Tafari's planes made good the threat. Into the massed ranks of Ras Gugsa's infantry, bombs and hand grenades were dropped. Terrified, the tribesmen broke and ran. Then Tafari's infantry fell upon them with the bayonet. The mass of the army ran in panic. Ras Gugsa and his bodyguard stood and fought to the end. At last a bullet struck Ras Gugsa in the throat and he fell to the ground and died.

Two days later, in Addis Ababa, the Empress Zauditu followed her ex-husband to the grave. She died, perhaps, of a broken heart.

For Tafari the moment was solemn. The body of the Empress rested in state. The throne of the Empire was his at last. It was the ambition that had burned in his heart since he had been a boy of seven, within the medieval walls of Harar. It was fulfillment of his father's dream. He moved his personal bodyguard into the palace and sat down at his simple desk to compose the following proclamation to the people of his country:

Proclamation in the name of the Crown Prince and Regent Plenipotentiary of the Ethiopian Realm, His Majesty, King Tafari Makonnen, on his ascending the Imperial Throne with the name of His Majesty Haile Selassie the First, King of the Kings of Ethiopia.

PROCLAMATION

King Tafari Makonnen

In accordance with the Proclamation which our Creator, abiding in his people, and electing us, did cause to be made, we have lived without breach of our Covenant as mother and son. Now, in that by the law and commandment of God, none that is human may avoid return to earth, Her Majesty the Empress, after a few days of sickness, has departed this life.

The passing of Her Majesty is grievous for myself and for the whole of the Empire. Since it is the long-standing custom that when a King, the Shepherd of his People, shall die, a King replaces him, I, being upon the seat of David to which I was betrothed, will, by God's charity, watch over you. Trader, trade! Farmer, plough! I shall govern you by the law and ordinance that has come, handed down by my fathers.

25 Megebit 1922 [3rd April 1930]

The proclamation finished, Tafari Makonnen bowed his head and asked his God for guidance. Then he went to his balcony and looked out over the city. He was thirty-seven, with a great lifetime before him, and he was Emperor of Ethiopia, from now on to be known to the world as Haile Selassie the First, Conquering Lion of the Tribe of Judah.

9

The Lion of Judah

Haile Selassie believed in liberty but he was not, where Ethiopia was concerned at least, a democrat. He knew that his people were too backward to govern themselves. They must be led out of the past and into the bright light of the modern day. To do this, Ethiopia needed a strong man at the top. Haile Selassie, from childhood, had believed that God intended him to be that man. He was a King, not a figurehead.

His coronation as King of Kings and Emperor of Ethiopia was an occasion of pomp and circumstance. Haile Selassie had his reasons for making the coronation impressive. He wanted to let the great powers of Europe know that a determined man now ruled the ancient mountain kingdom, and he wanted to impress the Rases with the fact that he was respected by the great governments of Europe.

Empress Zauditu died on April 2, 1930. Forty days of mourning passed, and then the rainy season began, so that until autumn Addis Ababa was a mud flat. The coronation was postponed until November 2.

For weeks, workmen labored to make the capital presentable. The mud road leading from the Palace to St. George's Cathedral was paved. The city police, though remaining barefoot, were put into smart-looking uniforms. The more offensive grog shops and other places of entertainment were closed. The Imperial Guard practiced ceremonial drill, old noncoms from the King's African Rifles teaching them the impressive slow march.

Haile Selassie supervised much of the work in person, driving out in his car to inspect the work on the new roads. He was fascinated by the modern equipment—steam shovels, rollers, asphalt melting machines.

At last the great day approached. From the

French Somali port of Jibuti, special trains carried official guests to the coronation. France sent a Marshal, complete with baton. Italy sent her Crown Prince. Representing King George V of Great Britain was His Royal Highness the Duke of Gloucester. From the surrounding British possessions, Kenya, the Sudan, Aden, British Somaliland, came a procession of high officials, admirals, and generals encrusted with gold braid, splendid in hats with ostrich feather plumes.

On the morning of November 2, as dawn broke over the eastern highlands and dew was fresh on the brilliant grass, the Archbishop Kyril anointed with holy oils the head of the new Emperor and upon it he placed the triple crown of the Ethiopian monarch. The Rases put on their coronets. They bowed to the new King of Kings, Negus Negusti. Then all over the city there burst into the morning air the roars and cheers of the people as the Emperor and his Empress marched beneath a series of triumphal arches. Army officers in full dress moved among the foreign guests, offering coronation medallions as souvenirs of the great occasion.

There was a banquet for the foreign guests, prepared by French chefs, and for a week, Addis Ababa went on a wild jamboree. There was raw meat for the soldiers and hundreds of gallons of sweet champagne. Barefoot soldiers sang in the streets and fired their rifles into the air. Pretty

Galla girls dressed in immaculate white shammas flirted with troops of the Imperial Guard, splendid in their caps made of lions' manes.

At last the foreign guests departed and the city settled down to its normal pace. The coronation was over. Had it been a success?

Haile Selassie had wanted to impress Europe and in part he had succeeded. The representatives of the great nations saw an intelligent and serious monarch, of elegant bearing and great self-confidence, speaking easily in French and English, at home in the world of affairs. They also saw a nation that seemed hopelessly backward.

The English novelist Mr. Evelyn Waugh was frankly contemptuous and seemed to feel that he had been visiting a land of cannibal kings. The London *Times,* most famous of all newspapers, wrote: "It is absurd to pretend that Ethiopia is a civilized nation in any Western sense of the word. Communications are hopelessly bad. A few miles outside Addis Ababa there is not a single motor road . . ."

And so on. For several columns, the *Times* went on to list the backwardness of the country, and its correspondent seemed to hold out little hope for improvement within the next generation or two.

The article was brutal, almost cruel. When he read what the *Times* had to say, Haile Selassie was hurt. From the Italians he expected contempt. From the French he accepted indifference. But he regarded the British as his friends and as the friends of his country.

"I must move at once. I must do something dramatic," he said. "We must prove to the world that we are more than a nation of black serfs and feudal barons."

Almost at once, Haile Selassie took a great step forward. In all history, since the days of the Bible, the people of Ethiopia had been bound to their feudal rulers, the Rases. They had no rights. With a stroke of the pen, Haile Selassie turned them into subjects of the state, in effect, citizens. He gave them a written constitution, the first in all of Ethiopian history. This was not done at the people's demand, but bestowed as a free gift of the Emperor.

The new constitution did not hand over power to the people, as does, for example, the constitution of the United States. The people were not ready for that. Few of them could read and write. Most of them knew nothing of the world, or even of Ethiopia beyond the borders of their own provinces. The Constitution of 1931, in Haile Selassie's mind, really established a school in which the people could learn to manage their own affairs. A student of Ethiopian history has called the 1931 Constitution, ". . . in fact, a rehearsal, or 'dry run' for a democracy to come."

The Emperor, of course, was Head of State. Under him served two Houses of Parliament: a Senate, chosen by the Emperor, and a Chamber of Deputies, chosen by the Rases and tribal chiefs.

"The members who will consult together in these chambers," Haile Selassie explained to his people, "will come from various provinces, chosen under the authority of the Emperor, until such time as the people have reached a degree of education and experience enabling them to make the choice themselves."

"Until such time . . ."

Yet the constitution was not window dressing. Haile Selassie meant in the end to lead his people to real self-government. As he brooded in his study night after night, often until the dawn was breaking over the eastern mountains, Haile Selassie saw a vision of the future, but he was also aware of the present.

Everything must be done. There must be created a "reliable cadre of educated men," a group of officials, teachers, doctors, engineers, lawyers, businessmen. They must be trained, and this would take years.

In the meantime, Haile Selassie needed help, and for this help he searched the world. As his adviser on foreign affairs he selected a Swede, de Virgin. To advise him in matters of law, he employed a Swiss. For interior affairs, particularly on the abolition of slavery, he found an Englishman, de Halpert. But of all the corps of foreign advisers who came to the aid of the Emperor, most important and most influential was an American, Everard Colson, who became Haile Selassie's Minister of Finance. Colson, trained in the American State Department, soon became Haile Selassie's most trusted adviser.

With these men at his side, Haile Selassie set himself to the task of remaking Ethiopia, step by step.

First, he broke the power of the Rases. They were ordered to remain in Addis Ababa, as advisers to the new regime. They remained in the capital, feasting and drinking, riding out to hunt lions for sport. In the meantime their private armies were broken up, and from the capital administrators and tax collectors were sent into their provinces. Haile Selassie was making a bid to centralize the country. He was working against time and he knew it. He needed ten, twenty years of peace, and the rumblings that were heard from Europe were not healthy, for the world or for Ethiopia. Hitler's brown-shirted troopers were smashing Jewish shops in Berlin. Mussolini was strutting on his balcony. In Japan, the generals were taking over the government. There was the smell of war in the air.

Still, Haile Selassie persisted.

Though he used foreign advisers in most of the important Cabinet posts, one office he kept for himself. That was the Ministry of Education. It is a job he holds today, and when an Ethiopian boy returns from abroad, after having studied at Oxford or Cambridge, Harvard or Yale or Columbia, it is the Emperor himself who puts him through his paces to see what he has done with his time.

The Rases grumbled at the loss of their power, but most of them accepted it. Not so Ras Hailu of Debra Marcos, capital of the ancient Kingdom of Gojjam. Through bribery, Ras Hailu arranged for Haile Selassie's old enemy, Lij Yasu, to make his escape from the castle at Fiche, where he was held in luxury as a royal prisoner. Disguised as a woman, Lij Yasu fled to the hills. Haile Selassie moved fast. Four days later, Lij Yasu was captured by government troops. He was still dressed as a woman, his eyes heavily painted with make-up. This time he was thrown into prison, a golden chain around his neck. The prison was a great stone castle at Harar, with high walls patrolled by government soldiers. In his stone chamber, locked away, Lij Yasu died insane and raving at the age of thirty-seven.

That was on November 22, 1935.

A few months later the Italian armies were in Harar. Had they found Lij Yasu alive, even though blubbering and insane, they could have used him as a figurehead for a Fascist regime in Ethiopia.

For Haile Selassie was not to get the ten years of peace he needed to put his country's house in order. The black legions of Benito Mussolini were to see to that.

10

Caesar in Abyssinia

"One day I will make the earth tremble," said Benito Mussolini to his mother, when he was a schoolboy with a satchel on his back.

The earth trembled only slightly. Ethiopia trembled to its very foundations.

After World War I, Italy, though one of the victorious nations, was disorganized and starving. Benito Mussolini, swaggering in the black-shirted uniform of his Fascist Party, made himself dictator of Italy and promised a return to the greatness of the days when ancient Rome ruled all the world. Mussolini was a violent man who had been a violent boy. He had been expelled from two schools for having knifed his classmates. "He picked quarrels for the sake of the fight," one of his biographers has written.

Compared with the French and the British, even with the Dutch and the Belgians, the Italians had few colonies. Mussolini was hungry for more. Italy controlled the strip of Red Sea coast called Eritrea, on the Ethiopian frontier. Mussolini wanted all of Ethiopia. At first he thought he could control the country by turning Haile Selassie into an Italian puppet. When he found that he was dealing with a brave and stubborn king, he decided that war was the only answer.

Suddenly, in the Italian newspapers (controlled by the government) there began to appear vicious attacks on Ethiopia and on Haile Selassie. Editorials in the Fascist papers suggested that what Ethiopia needed was the direction of a "civilizing power." And Marshal de Bono, one of Mussolini's most important soldiers, was sent to Eritrea to look over the situation at first hand.

"There must be war," de Bono reported to Mussolini. "And money will be needed, Duce. Lots of money."

"There will be money," Mussolini replied.

For weeks the Italians prepared for war, moving troops, bribing tribes on the Ethiopian border. It was clear that Mussolini meant to attack.

What was the attitude of the other nations of Europe, all members of the League of Nations, all pledged to defend Ethiopia should she be attacked?

The answer makes a shameful page in history. The great powers were afraid. The British wanted to prevent Mussolini from joining forces with Hitler and the Germans. To avoid this, one commentator says, the British Foreign Secretary "would have sold his own grandmother." The French, too, were concerned with Hitler's rise. They remembered the blood they had shed in World War I. The Americans were far away and in any case not members of the League.

As the war clouds gathered in Europe, Ethiopia stood alone, but Haile Selassie refused to believe it. He had faith in the League of Nations. He believed that England and France would come to his aid.

He was mistaken. The great powers that later sacrificed Austria and Czechoslovakia rather than risk offending the Germans, certainly would not interfere to defend Ethiopia, a faraway nation of dark-skinned people.

There was a border clash at a place called Wal Wal between Italian troops and an Ethiopian patrol. There were a hundred Ethiopian dead and wounded. About twenty Italians were killed.

At once Haile Selassie appealed to the League of Nations. A commission was appointed to investigate. It consisted of two Italians, one Frenchman, and one American. Needless to say, it reached no decision, though Wal Wal had always been considered Ethiopian territory and the Italians were clearly wrong.

Haile Selassie might have taken the Wal Wal incident as a lesson in what to expect from the League of Nations. He and his country were alone and helpless and about to be devoured. In Rome Mussolini smiled and studied maps with his field marshals. Italian crowds cheered in the streets: "Doo-chay! Doo-chay! Doo-chay!" Little boys with sharp daggers—the Fascist Boy Scouts, or *Balilla* —played at war with the Ethiopians.

Mussolini knew that he was safe. Secretly, the French and the British—Sir Samuel Hoare and the notorious Pierre Laval—agreed that they would not interfere, once Italy had started her conquest of Ethiopia. And through the Suez Canal, controlled by France and Britain, there moved heavily armed Italian divisions, equipped with the most modern instruments of war—tanks, artillery, armored cars, rapid-firing rifles, endless convoys of motor transport. They were the Legions of the modern Caesar, ready to pounce on a helpless nation.

At last, in desperation, Haile Selassie mobilized the Ethiopian Army. That is to say, he put the regiments on a fighting basis and moved them into defensive positions. The Italians took this as a signal to attack, and in force. The Fascist divisions moved across the border from the Italian colony of Eritrea into Ethiopian territory.

The invasion had begun.

Haile Selassie's tribesmen were confident. Too confident. Their fathers had beaten the Italians at Adowa a generation ago. They would do the same today. For two thousand years and more they had been safe in their mountains, protected by one of the greatest natural fortresses in the world. They were not afraid and their hearts beat faster when the war drums sounded at the gate of the Menelik Palace. It was the second of October, 1935.

"The Italian armies have crossed the Mareb River," the proclamation announced. "We are at war."

Cheers rose from the crowds; the hearts of the people were brave. But courage was not to be enough against tanks and artillery and aircraft.

And courage was not to be enough against skilled modern generals. Mussolini sent his best commanders to fight against Haile Selassie. In the north the Fascist armies were commanded by Marshal de Bono. The southern forces were led by General Graziani. On the airstrips in Eritrea, newly constructed by Italian army engineers, were three hundred modern aircraft. Haile Selassie's "air force" consisted of half a dozen planes. And in the ammunition dumps behind the Italian lines were thousands of cylinders of poison gas, the deadly, painful mustard gas last used in World War I.

The Italian campaign was swift and ruthless. Marshal de Bono was a gentleman soldier of the old school. When he refused to use mustard gas against the Ethiopians, he was relieved of his command. In his place, Mussolini sent a tougher commander, Marshal Badoglio. Badoglio was not so sentimental. To him, the dark-skinned Ethiopians were animals. Soon the sleek Italian planes were spraying the ground with mustard gas, scorching the feet of the barefoot troops, blistering their lungs. The true horror in all its detail Haile Selassie later described in his speech to the League of Nations.

Meanwhile, in the capitals of Europe, the League's great powers sat and did nothing when they read the reports. Haile Selassie shook his head.

"Don't they understand that they are preparing their own destruction?" he asked.

In London, certain others were making the same observation. Sir Anthony Eden (now Lord Avon) fought to get arms for Haile Selassie. He failed. And Winston Churchill wagged his head. He had predicted all of this and tried to warn his own government. "We could have stopped Musso," he said. "We made Musso a great power."

Halfheartedly, the League of Nations protested against the Italian invasion, but the member states had no intention of interfering with Mussolini's advance. Mussolini shouted and blustered, stood on his balcony in Rome, hands on his hips, face lifted to the sky, and defied the world, while his armies continued the massacre.

What of the Ethiopian armies?

"I am no soldier," Haile Selassie once had said.

It was true. He was a builder, a man of peace and a man of law. He was brave enough, but he had no gift for the management of war and his top field commander, Ras Mulegeta, was an Ethiopian war lord of the old school. He was brave, reckless, and ignorant.

The Italians moved easily into Adowa, where their fathers had been defeated by Menelik, and into Axum, where in ages past the Kings of Ethiopia had been crowned. They used their tanks and aircraft, and they used another weapon—treason. The Italians had bought one of Haile Selassie's field commanders, Gugsa, a young drunkard who felt he had been slighted by the Emperor. Gugsa not only failed to oppose the Italians with his ten thousand riflemen, but he provided them with the maps they needed to continue their advance.

As the Italians moved forward, Ras Mulegeta, the Minister of War, prepared to meet them at

Amba Aradam, a table-topped mountain five miles long, 9,000 feet above sea level. With him, the old war lord had the flower of Haile Selassie's army. Marshal Badoglio, the Italian commander, knew that if he could crush Mulegeta here the rest of the war would be an Italian parade to Addis Ababa.

The Italians threw everything they had into the battle. For hours, heavy artillery blasted the mountain top. Wave after wave of light bombers swept across the plateau, strafing with machine guns after they had dropped their bombs. And up the steep cliffs of Amba Aradam, using ropes and rock axes, came regiments of Alpini, crack Italian mountain infantry, with ostrich plumes in their tall hats. When they reached the plateau, the Alpini troopers fell on Ras Mulegeta's forces from the rear. The old warrior looked toward the sky and shook his fist. A low-flying Italian plane swooped toward him, guns blinking in the high, rare air. The old war chief fell dead. Around him, in panic, his army broke and ran.

"Our casualties in the Battle of Amba," Marshal Badoglio reported to Mussolini, "including dead and wounded, were 36 officers, 621 Italians, and 145 native troops."

Ras Mulegeta's army lost 20,000 men in the battle. It was not war any longer, it was mechanized slaughter: barefoot men, armed with spears and old rifles, against one of the most modern armies in the world, backed by a ruthlessly efficient air force, stubborn old Rases against Italian generals who were skilled technicians.

"It isn't a war. It isn't even slaughter," wrote Dr. John Melly of the British Ambulance Service. "It's the torture of tens of thousands of defenceless men, women and children with bombs and poison gas. They are using gas incessantly and we've treated hundreds of cases, including infants in arms. And the world looks on—and passes by on the other side."

Dr. Melly later was killed, one of a number of foreigners who gave their lives for the Ethiopian cause.

In Addis Ababa, Haile Selassie watched his armies disintegrate. The dreams for his country, held since childhood, were burning to death on the high plateau at Amba Aradam. Betrayed by the League of Nations, refused arms by the British, whom he had thought were his friends, he stood alone in his capital, ignored by the world.

He understood that the war was lost, but he knew that he must fight on to the end. If he gave up now, he would forever lose the respect of the Rases and of the tribesmen in the hills. He would lose his crown. And he had faith that was lacked by the men in striped trousers who sat in London and Paris.

He believed that in the end God would see that justice was done and that one day the Italian invaders would be driven from his country.

"I will mobilize the Imperial Guard and go to the front," he told Waizero Menen. "The soldiers must see their Emperor."

The Imperial Guard, 5,000 well-trained riflemen, were the only truly disciplined troops in the Empire. They had been trained by a Swedish professional and they marched and drilled like a European force. With Haile Selassie in the lead, this column marched toward the front, 30,000 tribesmen behind them. To face the Italians, Haile Selassie had with him one battalion of artillery, the guns served by half-trained men. The Italians had not given him the time to train and equip the army he needed.

To the world and to his wife, Haile Selassie offered a brave and self-confident front. Privately, he had no hope. To his boyhood friend Ras Imru, he wrote: "Hold your position if you can. If you think it better to come here and die with us, let us know your decision."

When he left Addis Ababa at the head of the Imperial Guard, Haile Selassie was prepared to die for his country. He had decided to attack the Italians at Mai Chow, where Badoglio's people were in camp, resting after their victories. Badoglio was ready for the attack. He moved up his best divisions, and in front of the Italian line of battle were strewn hundreds of thousands of fragments of broken glass. From his observation post in the hills, through field glasses, Haile Selassie saw the shards of glass glinting in the bright mountain sunlight. He glanced around him at his barefoot soldiers.

In his field tent, at a folding table, the Emperor studied his battle maps, working out the plan of attack. His object was to prove to the world that he and his men were brave, for there was no hope of winning.

On the night of March 30, orders were passed, and at dawn the next morning the first of the Ethiopian patrols made contact with Badoglio's advance units.

The battle had started.

Wave after wave of dark-faced soldiers were sent against the Italian positions. They fought bravely. Even Badoglio, when he reported to Mussolini, praised the "remarkable degree of training, combined with a superb contempt of danger," of the men of Haile Selassie's Imperial Guard. In the heat of the battle, Haile Selassie himself manned a machine gun, firing short quick bursts into the Italian ranks.

The bravery of the Imperial Guard was not enough. Alpini marksmen and several regiments of Black Shirt Militia cut to ribbons the advancing

Ethiopian formations. By evening it was clear that Haile Selassie's offensive had failed. He radioed the following message to the Empress in Addis Ababa:

From five in the morning until seven in the eve-ning, our troops attacked the enemy's strongest posi-tions. We also took part in the action and by the Grace of God remained unharmed. [He had, in fact, time after time exposed himself to Italian fire in an effort to inspire his men.] Our chief and trusted com-manders are dead or wounded. The Guard fought magnificently and deserve every praise. Our troops, even though they are not adapted for fighting of the European style, were able to bear comparison throughout the day with the best of the Italian troops.

His message to the Empress was hopeful, but Haile Selassie knew that when the attack failed, all hope for a successful defense of Ethiopia was gone. It had been a forlorn hope at best. Now his armies were falling back in disorder, leaving guns and rifles behind them. The skies darkened and soon the heavy clouds burst. Rain poured down, turning the mountainsides into quagmires. At this moment Marshal Badoglio began his counterattack. His tough mountain infantry, trained on the high slopes of the Alps, drove the Ethiopian Army before them through the mud, until soon there was no army, but only a mass of terrified men, women, children, ani-mals, all running hysterically. Stolidly through the rain, sliding on the slippery mule tracks, Haile Selassie moved back with the army. For the first time, lack of hope struck deep at his heart and spirit. His mind seemed no longer able to function. Like his men, he was suffering from the shock and fatigue of battle, and he felt a mindless desperation. He yearned for the help of his God.

"I will go to Lalibela," he decided. "I will ask for guidance from the Almighty."

It was Easter when the Emperor reached Lalibela, one of the holiest places in Ethiopia. Here, hewn from solid rock, are eleven churches, connected by underground rock passages, so that in fact the entire mountain is a vast underground cathedral. It is difficult to imagine a spot on this earth where a man is more removed from the affairs of daily life. Here, in the chill darkness of Lalibela, while water dripped slowly from the red rock walls and hundreds of candles flickered like stars, Haile Selassie remained for two days, fasting and praying. All his life the Emperor had been a deeply religious person, but never, one must believe, had his soul been closer to God than during those two days at Easter time, when he prayed at Lalibela.

On the fourteenth of April, Haile Selassie joined the remnant of the once proud Imperial Guard. Their uniforms were in tatters. Many were wounded. Many had lost their rifles. They were exhausted. But they were loyal. With them the

Emperor marched to Dessye, the old capital of Ras Mikael. In the now clear skies overhead, Italian fighter planes whirled lazily in the air.

"The Italians will be in Dessye by evening," the Emperor decided. "We must press on."

The tired soldiers resumed the march. A few days later, Haile Selassie reached the mud village of Fiche, connected by road to Addis Ababa. A car was found and the tired Emperor climbed into the back seat. Through the night, over the rutted mud road, he drove to the capital, an exhausted and defeated man, but proud.

11

The long road to exile

In the great hall of the Imperial Palace at Addis Ababa, the Rases of Ethiopia sat in council. Badoglio's army was making its way toward the capital.

"The war is lost," Haile Selassie told the Rases. "We have been betrayed by our friends and by the League of Nations. Our army is finished. Soon the Italians will be here in Addis Ababa. But I do not propose to give up. I will go into the Gojjam country and begin to raid against the Italian garrisons. We will fight from the hills, from the gorges of the Blue Nile."

Ras Kassa rose to his feet. He was an old ally and a true friend. "With all due respect to Your Majesty, what he proposes is madness."

"Ras Kassa is right," Waizero Menen said. "You must go to Geneva and appeal to the League of Nations."

The Emperor argued. The Rases listened. At last they took a vote. By twenty against three they gave their opinion: Haile Selassie should leave the country and go to the League in Geneva.

Haile Selassie's face hardened. "Have Menelik's drum brought into the courtyard," he commanded. "We will see what the people think."

For two hours the great war drum of Menelik boomed out its message in the courtyard of the Palace. Overhead, Italian war planes droned, flying in circles above the city. They did not bomb the capital because of the thousands of Europeans, many Italians among them, who had been caught there by the invasion.

Into the Palace courtyard came the army commanders from all over Addis Ababa. Most of them had been in the fighting, and some bore the scars of combat.

"I want volunteers," Haile Selassie told them. "Five thousand men to defend the capital and hold up the Italian advance, while I lead a guerrilla force to the mountains in the west."

Men surged forward, rifles and sabers raised in the air. Haile Selassie gave instructions that a banquet be prepared for them. "I am proud of you," he said. "Wait for my orders."

The orders to defend the capital were never given. When he returned to the great hall of the Palace, the Empress and Ras Kassa finally persuaded Haile Selassie that his position was hopeless, that for the good of the country he must make an appeal to the League of Nations.

His instinct was to fight, for he came from a long line of fighting kings, but he saw the wisdom of his wife's position and that of Ras Kassa. What would be served if he shed even more of the people's blood? What would be served if he stopped a bullet and died in the high hills of the Gojjam?

"Very well," he agreed at last. "I will go to Geneva. I will put our case before the world."

A correspondent who watched Haile Selassie come out of the Palace after making his decision to go into exile has described him thus:

"He was dressed in khaki as a general. His aspect froze my blood. Vigor had left his face and as he walked forward he did not seem to know where he was putting his feet. His body was crumpled up. His shoulders drooped. The medals on his tunic concealed a hollow, not a chest."

It was the low point of his life. He crossed the courtyard and his long thin fingers touched Menelik's war drum, caressing the taut skin. He felt that he had failed his ancient line that reached back to King Solomon. With a broken heart he went back into the Palace and joined the Empress. How her heart must have ached to witness the grief of the man she loved!

On May 2, 1936, in the late afternoon, with the sun turning toward the western mountains from which he had hoped to fight on, Haile Selassie began his long journey into exile. With him were the Empress, his three sons, his two daughters, and several of the leading Rases. The special train made its way across the Danakil Desert, a few hours ahead of the first Italian patrols, armored cars from Marshal Graziani's army of the south, their radio masts lashing the air like whips.

In Addis Ababa, all government was gone, and all hope. The soldiers looted the liquor shops and lurched drunkenly through the streets. They raped and murdered Europeans and smashed the European shops. They invaded the Palace and smashed the furniture. They shot the royal lions. They became a mob, a dangerous mob, and when Marshal Badoglio's advance columns entered Addis Ababa, the Italian commander was able to say with some justice that he had come to restore order to the unhappy capital.

At Jibuti, on the French Red Sea coast, Haile Selassie stepped aboard the British cruiser *Enterprise*. Sideboys in spotless white saluted as he passed between their files. A boatswain's pipe gave its eerie screech. A detachment of Royal Marines came smartly to attention at the command, "Present arms!" The ship's saluting gun boomed out the royal salute.

He was given a king's greeting. But on the foredeck of the sleek gray cruiser, British sailors shook their heads. "Poor little beggar," they said to each other. "He'll never see his own bloody country again. Old Musso has done him in properly."

"And 'oos's next on the blinkin' list?" some ordinary seaman must have asked.

For the common people of the world, the simple people, saw what their leaders refused to see: that the Fascist hunger for conquest would not be satisfied with crumbs. The sad, tired King who stepped aboard the *Enterprise* at Jibuti should have served as a warning to the world that Hitler and Mussolini and the Emperor of Japan would not rest until between them they controlled the entire surface of the earth. Little Ethiopia was only a beginning.

As the *Enterprise* steamed through the Mediterranean, bearing the Emperor to exile, there was cheering in Rome, where Mussolini appeared on his balcony to proclaim to the world that the King of Italy was now an Emperor and to warn the world that the days of Caesar and the Roman Legions had returned in modern dress. The victorious general, Marshal Badoglio, was appointed Viceroy of Ethiopia and the country was officially annexed to Italy.

In London, Stanley Baldwin, the British Prime Minister, heaved a sigh of relief. The Ethiopian crisis was over. "If only the little man will be quiet," he is supposed to have said, referring to Haile Selassie.

But Haile Selassie had no intention of going into silent exile in order to please Stanley Baldwin. In Jerusalem, where he was deliberately snubbed by the British High Commissioner, he sat in the drawing room of his suite at the King David Hotel. With the aid of his advisers, chief among them the American, Everard Colson, he drew up the appeal to the League of Nations with which we have opened this account of his life. And on May 10, 1936, the Secretariat of the League received his telegram, demanding that Ethiopia's case be heard.

He made his appeal to the League of Nations, and it will be recalled that when he left the platform he said softly, "It is us today. It will be you tomorrow."

How right he was!

He went to England, where he had been offered asylum. And one by one the nations of the world gave their answers to his plea for justice. Among the great states of the world, almost all were quick to accept Mussolini's conquest of Ethiopia. Only the United States, Mexico, New Zealand, and the Soviet Union refused to recognize the Italian invasion as legal. For the American action, Haile Selassie has always been grateful, and in the years that followed, it was often to the United States that he was to turn for advice and help when he needed them most.

12 *Exile and return*

It was in the pleasant city of Bath, in England, that Haile Selassie went into exile. A home was bought —Fairfield—and the greenhouse was turned into a chapel of the Coptic Church. Here, in the unfamiliar English light, filtered through heavy panes of glass, Haile Selassie and his Empress offered their daily prayers to God.

There was not much money. The state funds had been blocked, and in order to live, it was necessary for Haile Selassie to sell off many of his personal possessions. The winter of 1937–38 was a bitter one in England, but the household was rationed to a single fire. Beside this the Empress huddled. She missed the sun of her native land and could not adjust to the English climate, a difficulty she shared with many others not born on the sceptered isle.

"If she remains in England she will die," the Emperor was advised by his physicians. "She must be sent to a warmer climate."

So, with a heavy heart, Haile Selassie parted from his beloved comrade, Waizero Menen. She was sent to an Ethiopian convent in Jerusalem. The Emperor's youngest son, Sahle Selassie, went to the Holy Land with his mother. Haile Selassie remained in England, where he could be close to world affairs.

In Ethiopia, meanwhile, the Italians were meeting with problems. They met them in true Fascist style, with bloodshed and murder. Marshal Graziani had succeeded Badoglio as Viceroy, and in 1937 an Ethiopian patriot attempted to assassinate him. The attempt failed, but the Italian reprisals were swift. Every student who had attended a university outside Ethiopia was shot. One hundred Coptic priests were executed. And, as the Black Shirts ran wild in the streets of Addis Ababa, more than six thousand ordinary citizens were murdered. Racial segregation was strictly enforced and Ethiopians were forbidden to use the bus services and taxis that were provided for the Italians.

The Ethiopians responded to this terror as one might expect a proud people to respond. In the high mountains, guerrilla bands were created almost spontaneously. They were to form a nucleus when the time came for real resistance. In the meantime they made life difficult for the conquerors. The new roads the Italians had built at great cost could be used only under armed escorts. The mineral riches they had hoped to take from Haile Selassie's mountains were not forthcoming. To the Fascist conquerors, Ethiopia was becoming a burden rather than an asset.

Each day Haile Selassie kept in touch with events in Ethiopia. He sent trusted agents into the country, brave men who risked death to meet with the hill tribes and the Rases. These men reported that the hill tribes were ready to fight, perhaps with more vigor now than when they had faced Badoglio, for now they understood what it meant to live under foreign rule and to be treated as members of an inferior race.

"We must wait," the Emperor said. "In the end the Italians will go too far. And they are tied to Hitler. He will lead them to ruin if they can't find the way themselves."

Of course the statesmen in London and Paris were to learn that "the little man"—the scorned

Ethiopian Emperor—had been right and that they had been wrong. The Fascists wanted the world, and in the autumn of 1939, when Hitler's armies invaded Poland, they started out to get it.

World War II had commenced.

Mussolini waited for a few months to be sure that he was on the winning side. Then, when France was reeling under the German attack, he declared war. His troops crossed into France, and in Africa they entered the Sudan and British Somaliland, countries bordering on Ethiopia. The die was cast. The little Emperor, tucked away in his refuge in Bath, was now a hero and a world figure.

In London, Britain had a fighting chief at last, and it was Winston Churchill himself who decided that Haile Selassie should play a leading part in the liberation of his country. At once, British officials met with the Emperor at Bath.

But there were other Englishmen in Cairo who had never lost faith in the Emperor or his people. One of these was Colonel Daniel Sandford, who had farmed in Ethiopia for many years. He and his wife were personal friends of Haile Selassie. With other British and Ethiopian comrades, Colonel Sandford formed the nucleus of what was to be known as Mission 101—a mission that intended, with the help of Haile Selassie, to throw the Italians out of Ethiopia.

To the fighting Rases in Ethopia, whose men

were already ambushing Italian patrols, Mission 101 sent the following message:

"Peace be unto you. England and Italy are now at war. We have decided to help you in every way possible to destroy the common enemy. If you are in need of rifles, ammunition, food or clothing, send as many men and animals as you can spare to the place our messengers will tell you. We can help you with your requirements. It would also be wise to send your personal representative to consult with us and to arrange the best means of attacking the common enemy."

The message was signed by General Sir William Platt, Commander-in-Chief of the Anglo-Egyptian Sudan, but the spirit behind it was that of Colonel Sandford. In return for this, after the war, Sandford was given the right to own land in Ethiopia, the only foreigner so honored.

In Bath the Emperor's servants closed forever the house of exile. In a blacked-out train from Paddington Station, the Emperor traveled to the south of England. He moved with the deepest secrecy and under a false name. A flying boat of the RAF—a Sunderland—carried him and his staff to Alexandria, in Egypt, where he paused on his way to Khartoum in the Sudan, from which place he intended to lead an army back into Ethiopia.

On his first night in Alexandria, the Emperor, with a representative of the British Foreign Office, walked down to the banks of the ancient Nile. He knelt beside the famous river, and the waters of the Nile flowed between his fingers.

"C'est l'eau de mon pays," he said in the soft Egyptian evening. "It is the water of my country."

He was thinking of Lake Tsana, headwaters of the Blue Nile, great inland sea of his country. He rose and walked back to his hotel, his heart filled with new hope.

He was eager to be on his way, but for a time difficulties were placed in his path. The British High Command in the Sudan raised questions of authority. Certain British diplomats even suggested that until the war was won in Europe Ethiopia remain Italian, and that Haile Selassie had no rights in his own country.

These problems were solved and Haile Selassie moved on to Khartoum, where he was housed in the Pink Palace, under heavy guard. There he waited.

Meanwhile, Colonel Sandford and his comrades in Mission 101 had entered the Province of Gojjam, where they were rallying the war lords. Haile Selassie itched to join the fight and he appealed directly to London. Sir Anthony Eden and General Wavell, Commander-in-Chief of the British forces in Africa, came to see the Emperor at Khartoum. After this conference, Haile Selassie was recognized as personal leader of the War of Liberation and thousands of Ethiopian tribesmen poured into the Sudan to volunteer in his service. They were organized into the Patriot Army. Soon these barefoot soldiers were drilling in the broiling sun of the Sudan, forming fours and marching to cadence under the bellowed commands of old-fashioned British sergeant-majors, tough men with leather lungs and ramrod backs who had passed all of their lives in the business of making soldiers.

Two British officers were selected to help and advise Haile Selassie. One was to become world-famous. He was Orde Wingate, then a major, and certainly one of the most curious soldiers ever to wear the King's uniform. Fearless and eccentric, he was almost a religious fanatic, fond of quoting scripture even when discussing military matters. He had certain odd habits. Instead of bathing in the usual way, he preferred to scrub his entire body with a toothbrush. Often he received visitors in the nude, an alarm clock dangling from his wrist. He was unimpressive physically, and his uniforms were untidy, the pockets of his tunic often unbuttoned. He was the opposite of the Hollywood concept of the spotless British officer, yet for the kind of war that was to be fought in the Ethiopian highlands, he was the ideal man for the job. He could improvise. He was inventive. He could cut through red tape. He was not afraid to argue with high authority.

And he was a man of honor. A passionate Zionist, though not himself a Jew, he believed in the rights of small nations. His face had the rough character of sculpture done in unpolished granite; his eyes were like bright blue stones. On his way to meet Haile Selassie for the first time, he sat in the aircraft, reading the Bible. One would like to know what passages he selected as food for his soul. After Ethiopia was liberated, he went on to fight in Burma and there he was killed.

In the Pink Palace at Khartoum, Wingate bowed before Haile Selassie.

"I bring you most respectful greetings, Sire. In 1935, fifty-two nations let you and your country down. That act of aggression led to this war. I come as adviser to you and the forces that will take you back to your country and your throne. We offer you freedom and an equal place among the nations. But it will be no sort of place if you have no share in your own liberation. You will take the leading part in what is to come."

It was a prepared statement, but Orde Wingate had prepared it. To the formal words he added a few of his own, and he gave his personal word to the Emperor that Ethiopia should have justice.

For the first time in almost five years, a true spark of faith flashed in the soft brown eyes of Haile Selassie. He felt in his bones that this odd British officer was a man he could trust. The trace of a smile touched his mouth.

"Thank you, Major Wingate," he said.

The next day Haile Selassie put aside the civilian clothes he had been wearing and dressed himself in starched khaki, scarlet tabs at the collar, a scarlet band on the peaked cap. It was the uniform of a general in the Ethiopian Army.

On the barrack square the ragged hillmen were being turned into modern soldiers. Haile Selassie's heart beat faster, though to the outward eye he retained the calm, almost timeless air of patience that had been since childhood one of his great political assets.

He did not have long to wait.

Advance units pressed forward, and as the noon sun stood high in the sky on January 20, 1940, Haile Selassie crossed the border from the Sudan and trod on Ethiopian soil once more. There was a simple ceremony. A flagpole had been erected not far from the river bank. After a blessing from the Itchege, or High Priest, Haile Selassie stepped forward with the quick step of a soldier and hoisted the red, green, and gold flag of his country to the top of the pole. It fluttered brightly in the sun, the Lion of Judah showing proudly in the center panel. There was a silence, then a dark-faced bugler sounded reveille. The Emperor stepped back, stood at attention, and saluted. A toast was drunk in warm beer, and the ceremonies were over. The real business was about to begin.

Through dense jungles and mountain passes,

country almost unmapped, Wingate and the Emperor led the Patriot Army toward the highlands of Belaya and the city of Debra Marcos. Doing thirty miles a day, they pushed through the jungle, camping often without water. The Emperor shared every hardship. When a lorry was stuck in the sand, Haile Selassie put a shoulder to the chassis with the others. He helped to lay stone tracks where the going was too rough for the trucks.

Meantime, from Kenya, South African soldiers drove north and entered Addis Ababa. Their commander, General Cunningham, asked Wingate to hold up Haile Selassie's advance. "There are 25,000 Italians in Addis Ababa," he said. "White people. If Haile Selassie arrives, the natives will panic. They will go wild and start looting and raping and the Italians will be killed. So keep the little man out."

Like many others, General Cunningham underestimated both Wingate and the Emperor. Wingate ignored the order and the Patriot Army pressed on. On May 5, Haile Selassie entered his capital in triumph. Wingate rode on a white horse. The Emperor rode in an Alfa Romeo picked up in Debra Marcos. In front of the Royal Palace, General Cunningham waited with an honor guard of the King's African Rifles. The day was mild and the air was filled with the perfume of the eucalyptus trees. The people of Addis Ababa were massed to greet their ruler. Haile Selassie raised his head and breathed deeply of his native air. Then he spoke softly to the crowd.

"Today is the beginning of a new era in the history of Ethiopia," he said. "Since this is so, do not reward evil for evil. Do not commit any act of cruelty like those which the enemy committed against us. Do not allow the enemy any occasion to foul the good name of Ethiopia. We shall take his weapons away from him and make him return by the way he came."

The crowds cheered. Soberly, the Emperor looked off at the range of mountains outlined against the ice-blue sky. He must have offered a silent prayer to God and to his native mountains. It was exactly five years to the day since the Italian armies had invaded Ethiopia.

13

The struggle for power

Had Orde Wingate remained in Ethiopia, much difficulty might have been avoided, but Wingate was a soldier and he followed the sound of the guns. He went on to Burma, where he fought in the jungles against the Japanese, and there he was killed. Haile Selassie became godfather to Wingate's only son, a gesture that had profound meaning to the Emperor, and today in Addis Ababa there stands the Orde

Wingate School, where instruction is given in English as well as Amharic.

With Wingate gone, after the liberation, only Daniel Sandford, by now a Brigadier, remained to support Haile Selassie against the British military commanders who wished to control the country, at least until the war in Europe had ended. Most of the British officials sent to Ethiopia were old-line colonial administrators from Kenya, the Sudan, South Africa, Rhodesia—men used to dealing with colered people as inferiors, almost as children.

There were clashes.

Haile Selassie's position was simple. The Italians had been defeated and he was back on the throne. His task was to rebuild the country. The British took a different view. There was the war in Europe to be won, and then the struggle in the Malay jungles against the Japanese. The Germans had sent an army to North Africa, under the famous General Rommel. The British insisted that their army retain a certain amount of control over Ethiopian affairs. One British official went so far as to say that since a peace treaty had not been signed, the King of Italy remained the legal ruler of Ethiopia.

Such are the convolutions of the ultra-legal mind!

Behind legality and military necessity there lurked a more sinister idea. Among the British there were those who hoped to add Ethiopia to Britain's vast African empire. Where the Italians had failed, these men thought a more enlightened British colonialism might succeed. Let Haile Selassie become a figurehead; true authority would come from London.

Haile Selassie was not the man to knuckle under, even to the British who had fought by his side. He was polite, always calm, but he was firm. The British were not so calm. White South African soldiers, drunk on bootleg whisky or the native *tej,* insulted Ethiopian officers and Rases. They had brought with them all the race prejudice for which South Africa is well known. Offences against Italian women which General Cunningham had feared would be committed by Ethiopians did occur, but it was the white soldiers who were offensive.

The situation was intolerable, and at last Haile Selassie decided to go straight to the top. He sent a cable to Winston Churchill, asking when a treaty between Britain and Ethiopia was to be signed. He got his answer promptly. Ethiopia was to have complete independence. The only restrictions would be those occasioned by strict military necessity. Winston Churchill made it clear that Haile Selassie was head of state.

The Emperor turned to the work of reorganizing his country and of repairing the damage done by the Italians.

But first of all there was the question of what to

do about the Italians. There were 70,000 Italians in Ethiopia, 30,000 of them in Addis Ababa. The rape and slaughter predicted by General Cunningham had not occurred, and the Italians wanted to remain in the country.

Haile Selassie wanted them too.

Almost all of his young technicians and engineers, even his skilled clerical workers, had been murdered by the Occupation Forces during the reprisals conducted by Marshal Graziani. Until he could train his own people, Haile Selassie needed the Italians to run the essential services: railways, hospitals, telephone service.

The British army decided, however, that the Italians must be expelled from Ethiopia, and British patrols began to round them up and herd them into prison camps. In Addis Ababa, services slowly ground to a stop. Sadly, the Emperor realized that his country once again must pull itself up by its own bootstraps.

But not quite.

In 1945, when the war in Europe was drawing to a close, an American warship stood off Suez. On the quarterdeck sat a smiling, self-confident figure, wearing his panama hat, cigarette in a long holder jutting from his mouth at a jaunty angle.

It was Franklin Delano Roosevelt, and he was prepared to listen to Haile Selassie's problems. One imagines the famous smile and the great warm

spirit that had inspired millions, and the lift the
visit to Roosevelt must have given the tired and
nearly desperate Emperor. Here was a friend, a
warm friend. There was an invitation to visit America as soon as the war was over. And there was
the promise of economic aid.

Roosevelt kept his word. An American economic
mission arrived at Addis Ababa and American
money poured into the country. With the help of
Trans World Airlines, Air Ethiopia was established
and planes bearing the red, green, and gold colors of
Ethiopia flew to the great cities of the world. American oil wells began to tap the riches under the
ground. Boys from schools such as Kansas State
and the Oklahoma Agricultural and Mechanical
Colleges went into the mud-hut villages to help
the Ethiopian farmers produce more on their hill
farms. American heavy machinery appeared. Roads
were built. Schools. Hospitals. A university. The
Americans helped to establish agricultural colleges
at Harar and Jimma.

The Americans helped. American money and machines made it possible to build up the country.
And American boys with blond crew cuts worked on
the highland farms. But Ethiopia remained independent, firmly in the hands of Haile Selassie.

The British were not pleased. They tried to prevent Ethiopia from signing the Treaty of Peace,
but Haile Selassie, with his American friends behind

him, insisted and Ethiopia signed with the other powers that had fought against Italy and Germany. (The British, in 1942, had tried, on legal grounds, to prevent Ethiopia from joining the United Nations, but the Emperor had been insistent then and Ethiopia is a Charter Member.)

Though he was no longer young and though he had borne the hardships of war and invasion, Haile Selassie placed himself on a schedule that would have killed most men. He worked for twenty hours a day and slept for three. The last hour was devoted to prayer, for seldom does Haile Selassie make an important move without seeking the guidance of God.

During the first few years, the Emperor's achievements were magnificent. The judicial system was reformed. Slavery was wiped out. Education was pressed forward on all levels, and offered to girls as well as boys. The power of the Rases was brought under the control of the central government. A State Police Force, numbering several thousand men, was formed to bring order to the outlying provinces. The constitution was revised and the people were given the right to vote.

The currency was completely reformed. In the old days, the only money that had any value were the Maria Theresa talers. During the Italian occupation, all kinds of money flooded the country— Egyptian piastres, East African shillings, rupees,

French francs, and, of course, Italian lira. With the aid of his American advisers, Haile Selassie created a new currency based on the American dollar. Ethiopian money was issued in notes of $1, $5, $10, $50, and $100. These dollars are backed by reserves of United States dollars, held by the State Bank of Ethiopia. It is a sound currency.

Though Haile Selassie is a man of peace, he realized that in this troubled world a nation must be protected by its own armed forces. A small but efficient army was built up, trained at first by Swedes, then by the British, then by an American military mission. It is armed with modern American weapons.

When the war in Korea broke out, Haile Selassie sent soldiers to serve with the forces of the United Nations. They served well.

"The First Kagnew Battalion, Imperial Ethiopian Expeditionary Force to Korea, is cited for outstanding performance of duty and extraordinary heroism in action against the enemy in the vicinity of Sam-Hyon, Korea, during the period of 16th September to 22nd September, 1951. . . ."

So reads in part the United Nations citation to the Ethiopian soldiers who fought in the rice paddies of Korea. They were cited again for their action in May of 1953:

"The superb *esprit de corps* and extraordinary heroism displayed by the members of this unit reflect great credit upon themselves, their organization, and the Ethiopian Army. . . ."

Haile Selassie had reason to be proud when he learned how bravely his men had fought beside the other troops of the United Nations, crack soldiers from the United States, France, Britain, and beside the brave South Koreans themselves. They must have remembered Adowa and the glory of their grandfathers; perhaps Haile Selassie thought of these things too, when he read the United Nations citations.

It was also during 1952 that Ethiopia regained her sea coast. The narrow strip of land along the Red Sea known as Eritrea had been controlled for years by the Turks and later by the Italians. When the Italians were driven out in 1941, a British administration was set up to govern the territory until the Treaty of Peace was signed. A United Nations Commission was appointed after the war was over, and finally, in September, 1952, the former Italian colony was made a federal part of Ethiopia, under the rule of Haile Selassie. The British Union Jack came down in the city of Asmara and in its place rose the three-barred flag bearing the Lion of Judah. After centuries as a land-locked nation, Ethiopia had a sea coast again and the great port of Massawah came under her control.

Haile Selassie made a state visit to Eritrea when the federation was proclaimed.

"By crossing the Mareb River," he told the crowds that welcomed him, "we are doing away with the barrier that has for so long separated brother peoples."

14

The Conquering Lion

One of Haile Selassie's regrets is that he was not to meet with Franklin Roosevelt for a second time, for of course the President died not long after he had visited with the Emperor at Suez. Haile Selassie never forgot the invitation extended by Roosevelt to visit the United States, but it was not until 1954 that things were sufficiently in order so that he could leave Ethiopia.

It was President Eisenhower who greeted him

when he came and stayed as a guest at the White
House, posing on the White House lawn in the manner of honored White House guests.

He wanted to see as much of America as his time
would permit, but the heads of protocol in the State
Department were faintly surprised when it was
asked that Stillwater, Oklahoma, be included on
the Emperor's tour of the United States.

The Emperor smiled and guessed at the question.

"So many of your young men from Oklahoma
A. & M. have come to my country to help my
people. I should like to see their college."

So, in addition to the great cities of Boston, New
York, Seattle, San Francisco, New Orleans, the Em-
peror journeyed to the town of Stillwater, on the
Oklahoma prairie.

He was impressed by what he saw in the United
States and impressed by the vigor of America.
One of the things that drew his keenest attention
was the Grand Coulee Dam on the Columbia River.
He looked at the great concrete barrage, the intricate
system of canals, and his mind turned to his own
Lake Tsana, at the headwaters of the Nile.

In Washington, Haile Selassie addressed a joint
session of the Senate and the House of Representatives. The Diplomatic Corps was present, the judges
of the Supreme Court, the President of the United
States. It was a moving speech. The Emperor

thanked the United States for the help his country had received and he expressed the love that he and his people will always have for the American republic.

His visit to the United States was only the beginning of Haile Selassie's travels abroad. A few months later he toured Europe. In London he was greeted by cheering crowds that lined the streets as he rode in the royal coach beside Her Majesty the Queen. In Paris, in Holland, in Scandinavia, he was received with respect and affection. And millions of those who cheered remembered the lonely figure who had stood before the League of Nations to plead for justice, the modest, proud, quiet-voiced King who had warned the world what to expect from Hitler and Mussolini.

He was in Brazil, during the winter of 1960, when his power was put to its bitterest test since the Italian invasion.

Not all of the Rases had really surrendered their power. It was the year of the Palace Revolt. The officers of the Imperial Bodyguard mutinied and reactionary leaders made an effort to get control of the government. The Emperor's son, Asfa Wossen, was forced to speak on the radio—with a pistol at his head—and to denounce his father's rule.

The rebellion did not have the support of the people. And the mass of the army backed Haile Selassie to a man. When he learned of the revolt, Haile Selassie flew at once from Brazil to Khartoum. From Khartoum he flew to Asmara, then on to Addis Ababa. He was greeted by a happy populace and by crack detachments of the army. The revolt collapsed.

The rebels first tried to flee, then two killed themselves. The third, General Mengistu, was tried for treason and hanged. The Crown Prince, Asfa Wossen, though innocent, bowed before his father and asked to be forgiven. He was forgiven.

The revolt, though it had no popular backing, had a profound effect on Haile Selassie. He is still very much an absolute monarch, in spite of the new constitution, which looks forward to eventual democracy, but he has begun to address his people on the radio, in the manner of American and European leaders, and to explain his policies with more care. He takes the people into his confidence more than he did in the early days.

Haile Selassie's last visit to the United States was not a happy one. In his full regalia, beside the other heads of state from all over the world, he marched to the slow beat of drums down Pennsylvania Avenue, following the caisson that carried President Kennedy's body.

Who knows what thoughts passed through his mind as he watched the martyred young President's last remains being borne to the Capitol Rotunda?

He was more than seventy, an old man, beyond

the Biblical span of years. President Kennedy had been cut down in the flower of his young life. He had been white and fair-haired. The Emperor is dark and brown-eyed, ruler of an Africa state. And yet there was much they had shared, the young dead hero and the old Emperor. Both of them had lived with passion and both had sought the good of mankind.

With a sad heart, when he turned away from a shocked and grief-stricken United States, Haile Selassie returned to Africa —to take up again the task to which he had given all the years of his long life —the stewardship of his native land and the care of the happiness of its dark-skinned people, free today and independent as they had been in the days of the Bible.

Bibliography

Rivalries in Ethiopia by Elizabeth P. MacCallum
World Peace Foundation, 1935

The Lion of Judah Hath Prevailed by Christine Sandford
Macmillan, 1955

Tropical Africa (*Life* World Library)
Time-Life Books, 1962

Ethiopia Under Haile Selassie by Christine Sandford
Dent, 1946

Haile Selassie by Leonard Mosley
Prentice-Hall, 1965

Abyssinia on the Eve by Ladislas Farago
London, 1935

Contemporary Ethiopia by David Abner Talbot
Philosophical Library, 1952

Africa's Last Empire by Hermann Norden
Macrae-Smith, 1930

Various issues of *National Geographic* Magazine

Material from Ethiopian Embassy

Survey of World Cultures (Ethiopia)
Human Relations Area Files, Inc. New Haven, Conn.